"Over the course of these ten ___ dig into the classic pillars of ___ also interrogates myriad other influences that contribute to his reality with an unflinching clarity, including class, intergenerational wealth and trauma, faith and fear, ambition and envy."
—ELENA PASSARELLO, author of *Let Me Clear My Throat* and *Animals Strike Curious Poses*

"Removing the veil of his own misconceptions and training a floodlight on those of our shared society, Franklin unpacks notions of goodness, nakedness, perception and—with a true vitality of language—confronts the myths we both inherit and perpetuate. All delusions aside, this is a work of greatness, grand in spirit and faith, willing to upend artifice and invention for the sake of empathy. This is a writer concerned with truth and healing, alive with a sober and dazzling sense of hope."
—JERICHO PARMS, author of *Lost Wax*

"With certainty undergirded by fact, and wisdom that never overreaches, these essays are grand (and not at all delusional)."
—DEBRA MONROE, author of *My Unsentimental Education*

"In the excellent essays of *Delusions of Grandeur*, Joey Franklin perfects, ages, then cures, perhaps, the genre's full extension and expression, engineering whole new worried and weathered precincts of prose genius. Here, the maturation of the micromemoir. Here, the fine calculus of the personal essay. Here, the literal reinvention of literary journalism. These big-shouldered essays are riveting, I beams bolted and bolting, hither and yon, spot lit and spot on."
—MICHAEL MARTONE, author of *The Moon Over Wapakoneta* and *Brooding*

"Joey Franklin dives into difficult topics—poverty and wealth, masculinity, race, whiteness, privilege, parenting, linguistic and regional bias, and what it means to be and do good in the world—with thoughtful grace. This book is a Montaignian mash-up relevant for twenty-first-century readers, each essay braided with equal parts fascinating research and deep vulnerability, an admirable union of brain and heart."

—SONYA HUBER, author of *Pain Woman Takes Your Keys, and Other Essays from a Nervous System*

DELUSIONS OF GRANDEUR

DELUSIONS

OF GRANDEUR

American Essays

JOEY FRANKLIN

UNIVERSITY OF NEBRASKA PRESS *Lincoln*

Acknowledgments for the use of copyrighted
material appear on pages ix–x, which constitute
an extension of the copyright page.

Library of Congress Cataloging-in-Publication Data
Names: Franklin, Joey, author.
Title: Delusions of grandeur: American
essays / Joey Franklin.
Description: Lincoln: University of Nebraska Press,
[2020] | Includes bibliographical references.
Identifiers: LCCN 2020016258
ISBN 9781496212108 (paperback)
ISBN 9781496224729 (epub)
ISBN 9781496224736 (mobi)
ISBN 9781496224743 (pdf)
Subjects: LCSH: Franklin, Joey. | National
characteristics, American. | United States—Politics
and government. | United States—Social conditions.
Classification: LCC PS3606.R42237
A6 2020 | DDC 814/.6—dc23
LC record available at
https://lccn.loc.gov/2020016258

Set in Adobe Garamond by Mikala R. Kolander.
Designed by N. Putens.

To Melissa and the boys,
for tempering all my delusions.

It were a foolish and ridiculous arrogance to esteem
ourselves the most perfect thing in this universe.

—MICHEL DE MONTAIGNE

It seems to me that life is much more important
than art. By which I do not mean that art is not
important, but it is only important because life is.

—JAMES BALDWIN

CONTENTS

Acknowledgments   *ix*

Delusions of Grandeur:
An Introduction   *1*

Toy Soldiers   *9*

Girl Fight   *31*

Good Enough   *34*

Stuck   *60*

White Trash   *77*

Not in My Backyard   *100*

Thursday Night Lights   *118*

The Full Montaigne   *125*

Worry Lines   *146*

Apocalypse, Now?   *160*

A Note on Notes   *187*

Notes   *189*

ACKNOWLEDGMENTS

To Melissa, for not running away all those years ago when she asked me what I wanted to do with my life, and I said *write*.

To Callan, Nolan, and Ian, for their deep curiosity and unwavering commitment to reminding me of all the hair I've lost and weight I've gained.

To my shaggy, raucous, divergent extended family and their loud mouths, open minds, and big hearts.

To the countless editors, colleagues, and friends who read early drafts and gave such helpful, frank advice: Patrick Madden, Lance Larsen, Spencer Hyde, John Bennion, Kristin Matthews, Jamie Horrocks, Dennis Cutchins, Rick Duerden, Kyle Minor, Jericho Parms, David Grover, Ryan Gabriel, Alicia Christensen, Shamae Budd, and Laura Julier, to name only a few.

Also, to the Brigham Young University Department of English for matchless academic support, and to the entire staff at the University of Nebraska Press for being such a delight to work with.

And, finally, to the editors and journals who first published the following essays:

"Girl Fight" first appeared in *Brevity*, no. 45 (Winter 2014), and was subsequently published in *The Best of Brevity*, edited by Dinty W. Moore and Zoë Bossiere (Rose Metal Press, 2020).

"Not in My Backyard" originally appeared in *Fourth Genre* 20, no. 1 (Spring 2018): 61–76.

"Stuck" first appeared in "The Masculinity Issue," *Hunger Mountain* (August 2015).

"The Full Montaigne" first appeared in *Ninth Letter* 12, no. 2 (Fall 2015): 57–65.

Thank you.

DELUSIONS OF GRANDEUR

Delusions of Grandeur

In high school my pal Eli drove a 1973 Oldsmobile Delta Royale 88—a jet-black coupe that stretched nineteen feet from bow to stern and weighed as much as an African rhino. It had cracked-vinyl benches you could sleep on comfortably, a trunk the size of a Jacuzzi, and carpet that smelled of vanilla air freshener and gasoline. In the mid-1970s, marketers called the Delta 88 a "tough cookie," but by 1996, Eli's 88 seemed more like a "moldy bran muffin." Still, Eli loved it, and I didn't have a car or a license, so I loved it too.

Eli spent his afternoons tinkering under the hood in his drive-way, and on Friday nights he'd pick up me and Tyler to go cruising around town like teenagers in some John Hughes film, slouched low, heads back, going nowhere fast. Tyler and I took turns riding shotgun and manning the radio while Eli steered the ship, and together the three of us rode the razor edge of something that felt like adulthood, convinced that real life waited somewhere out beyond the strip-mall borders of our suburb. A dangerous life of lead-foot lane changes and late-night burger runs where other boys scowled at us from their minivans and Honda Civics, and all the girls lined up for rides around town. A life where the rumble of that Rocket V8 would be the only calling card we'd ever need. A life that might have felt more ironic if we'd read some T. C. Boyle.

Delusion came easy enough back then, so preoccupied with tomorrow and what it would take to get there, thwarted by the slow drip of time and the irksome reality that adulthood required more than a few semesters of high school and a minimum-wage job. If we couldn't grow up any faster though, a couple of hundred horsepower could at least help us imagine ourselves into the future. Not that we ever succeeded at much more than driving circles around town and occasionally squeezing that 88 through the drive-in at Burger King. And we certainly never had girls lining up for any rides. But when I sat in that front seat, looking out on the world from a window as wide as the horizon, everything seemed possible, even the notion that someday we might become men.

By the time you read this, I'll have reached forty, which may be, in an era of delayed adolescence and misguided trust in stretch-fabric skinny jeans, the only undeniable evidence that I've finally become a man. And while I've largely outgrown any smug satisfaction that might come from a Nixon-era muscle car, my penchant for delusion hasn't much diminished. Sure I happily drive a minivan every day, but even the banal comforts of life in the middle class can be a source of undue satisfaction—a certain pride in my mort-gaged home and chain-link fence, in my ivory-tower teaching job and my relatively functional nuclear family—the lucky choice of a compatible (read: forgiving) mate and three healthy sons who are (mostly) happy to see me when I come home. It's not hard to think of even my late-model minivan as a sign that I've somehow arrived (nothing says "I've made it" quite like a Dodge Caravan with Stow 'n Go® seats).

In my wiser moments though, I'm aware that the only place I've arrived at is persistent debt, overscheduled kids, and a nagging feeling that the Joneses I've been struggling to keep up with are figments of our collective imagination. And even when I'm not feeling particularly wise, I know that a minivan is nothing to strut about (though, really, have you tried Stow 'n Go® seating?). And yet I manage to transform even mundane blemishes into something to brag about. The thirty-five pounds I've put on since my late twenties—I prefer to think of it as maturity weight. A family tree full of scoundrels—that's writing material. Parenting failures, childhood missteps, persistent bad habits—all important ingredients in creating what I like to call my lovable eccentricities. Self-deception serves nicely as a defense mechanism against the fact that most of us have no idea what we're doing.

Still, as apprehensive as I feel about my own delusions, I might feel even worse if delusion weren't humanity's common lot. You and I are members of a species that brawls at Little League baseball games and permits the honor killing of children; that disowns family members for quitting church or joining the wrong one, for marrying across racial lines or coming out of the closet, for having an abortion or voting for the wrong candidate. A species that can raise a billion dollars in a few days to rebuild a burned-out cathedral in France but struggles to provide food for hungry children; a species that puts sexual predators in high office and our elderly in group homes; that dumps fast-food trash in parking lots, litters movie theaters with popcorn and empty soda cups, and is happy to let Greenland melt into the ocean if it means we can keep driving minivans and eating cheap hamburgers. Across the planet we conflate militarism with patriotism, and here at home we shrug off the deaths of children in mass shootings as just another cost of living in a free country. We thrive on clannish myths and convenient fantasies, and to protect them, we swallow whole streams of fake news and bask in the glow of endless partisan pandering. We deny science, cherry-pick history, and then imagine that in our dogged pursuit of self-interest, we'll still manage, somehow, to make the world a better place.

Pick your prophet, and the fundamental truth is the same. Solomon has "seen all the works that are done under the sun; and, behold, all is vanity." The apostle Paul tells us "men shall be lovers of their own selves." Muhammad? "What is the worldly life except the enjoyment of delusion." The Buddha? "Humankind is possessed by delusion, bound by delusion and delighted with being." More recently, Mary Wollstonecraft warned of "a deluge of false sentiments and overstretched feelings, stifling the natural emotions of the heart." Kierkegaard: "There are two ways to be fooled. One is to believe what isn't true; the other is to refuse to believe what is." W. E. B. Du Bois: "There is but one coward on earth, and that is the coward that dare not know." John Lennon described this as living easy "with eyes closed"; it's what made David Bowie "Afraid of Americans," and it's the reason Maya Angelou declared "It is possible and imperative that we learn / A brave and startling truth."

In our nobler moments of clarity, we are conscious of the human inclination to place ourselves at the crystal center of everything. But moments of clarity come so infrequently, and in the meantime, delusion is such an easy drug. And twenty-first-century discourse isn't helping the matter. Whether its profit-hungry cable news, the rage machine of social media, or the trench warfare of ideological isolationism, it is entirely too easy to preen our feathers and regurgitate our various tribal doctrines, instead of engaging in the hard, humbling work of understanding each other (and ourselves). Which brings me to the personal essay—a curious, unassuming literary form with a predilection for skeptical self-examination, a firm conviction in the value of personal experience, and an abiding devotion to the interconnectivity of people and things. A genre that, at its best, contains all the necessary ingredients for a clear-headed engagement with the complicated nature of human life.

Not that simply reading or writing an essay will magically transform any of us into saints of self-awareness. In the sixteenth century, when Michel de Montaigne, father of the modern essay, wrote, "I have no other end in this writing, but only to discover myself," he was quick to call his work "vain and frivolous" and admit that essaying was, altogether, a "thorny undertaking." In 1750 Samuel Johnson confirmed, "If it be reasonable to estimate the difficulty of any enterprise by frequent miscarriages, it may justly be concluded that it is not easy for a man to know himself"; and by 1905 Virginia Woolf had suffered through enough vapid, egocentric essayists to write, "Confronted with the terrible spectre of themselves, the bravest are inclined to run away."

Certainly I am as inclined as anyone to run away from uncomfortable truths, but for too long, delusional thinking has been killing us softly, one narcissistic fairy tale at a time. As I approach middle age, I find myself less enamored of convenient myths and more willing to accommodate those uncomfortable truths—especially if they carry the promise of a little clarity. And if there is a genre that can handle the pitch and yaw of discomfort, it's the essay. Can too much be said for this quirky, eccentric literary gift discovered by the ancients, distilled and named by Montaigne from the quiet of his chateau tower, and developed by modern practitioners into a genre as accommodating to activists and philosophers as to artists and storytellers—a genre that feels as at home in poetry as it does in prayer and demands only sincerity, humility, and curiosity as the price of admission? "Essays are restless literature," writes Rebecca Solnit. They show us "how the personal and the public can inform each other, how two overtly dissimilar things share a secret kinship, how intuitive and scholarly knowledge can cook down together, how discovery can be a deep pleasure."

In a 1961 essay titled "The Discovery of What It Means to Be an American," James Baldwin writes, "The time has come, God knows, for us to examine ourselves, but we can only do this if we are willing to free ourselves of the myth of America and try to find out what is really happening here." Frankly though, I have no idea how to free us all from the convenient, painful, persistent myths and delusions that dominate American life. I have no easy solution for the evils of systemic racism and sexism, no chemical treatment for the cancers of toxic masculinity or political partisanship, no easy alternative to the dangers of religious dogma, nor a ready reply to baby-out-with-the-bathwater rejections of faith; no twelve-step plan to cure human arrogance about our place in the natural world, and no clue how we might finally convince ourselves that our care for one another must extend beyond the edges of our cultural, racial, and political borders. But I believe Baldwin when he says that we must examine ourselves, and I believe him when he says that we can't do that without first confronting our myths. So in the spirit of taking on Baldwin's challenge, I offer you this book—ten restless attempts to tackle my own mythologies, ten examinations of my own delusional thinking, each an effort to excavate a little public truth from my private reality. They're built from anxieties that won't go away and from memories that keep rising to the surface, and they're grounded in my own questions about what it really means to be a citizen, a parent, a child, a neighbor, a human being holding fast to the earth as it spins along out here on the edge of everything. Of course, I harbor no delusion that any of this is going to change the world, but it has certainly changed me, and if Baldwin is right, then that's at least a start.

More than twenty years have passed since the last time I went for a ride with Eli and Tyler in that old Delta 88. And when I think back on those long Friday nights we spent driving circles around our adolescence, one memory stands out among the rest. The three of us had made plans to visit a girl named Rochelle who lived in a big house near the top of Bull Mountain Road, but the 88's electrical system refused to cooperate. The dash lights flickered, and the radio signal faded in and out, and if one of us rolled down a window to combat the smell of vanilla and gasoline, the lights would dim as the battery drained itself dead. We should have simply stayed put, but the night was clear and there was a woman to impress, so we jumped the battery and headed out into the night—promising ourselves we'd drive slow and keep our hands off those window controls.

I don't recall much of the visit with Rochelle—an hour maybe parked at one end of an expansive driveway, vying for the affection of a girl who resided so definitively out of my league and tax bracket—but I will never forget the ride home. We climbed back into Eli's 88 and waved to Rochelle as we pulled out of her driveway. The air inside was thick and pungent, and without thinking I pressed the button to lower my window. The lights around us faded to black, the engine stalled, and the car began a free fall toward the bottom of Bull Mountain Road. Somebody laughed, somebody said, *uh-oh*, and Eli tried the ignition, but the power was gone, the brakes had turned to sponge, and the steering stiffened like we were driving through deep sand. In the darkness, the Delta 88 picked up speed, my stomach turned, and Eli tried the ignition again—nothing.

I remember briefly entertaining the thought, *We are going to die*, and somebody said *What do we do?* and somebody else said, *I bet we can make it*, and all of us were thinking about the hard right turn at the bottom of the hill and how fast we were heading toward it. Of course, I'm still here to write this story down, so you don't have to guess that we survived. At the height of our crackling uncertainty and wide-eyed panic, the car's electricity showed a few signs of life, and somebody said, *Pull over*. Eli tugged on the wheel, pressed hard into the brakes and rolled us to a stop against the curb. Somebody laughed again, and somebody said, *We should call my dad.* And then Tyler's parents came to pick us up, and we rode off into the night, leaving that old 88 to sit empty in the dark.

But balanced briefly on the cusp of that moment, when plowing through the hedge and fence and house at the bottom of the hill still felt like a poignant possibility, and without the luxury of knowing we would all live to laugh about it later, the full façade of the evening fell away, and the absurd reality of the situation appeared before me like a talisman. There we were, gripping the vinyl seats as we careened down a hill toward our collective ends in a car we had no business driving, all so I could chase a girl that I had no business chasing. We were not the indestructible teenagers we had supposed; the universe could, as it fancied, flip a switch and crash us all headlong through the rhododendrons and cedar fencing of some unsuspecting suburbanite. This was a cold, uncomfortable truth. But it was also a glimpse of things as they really were and a first inkling of what lies at the heart of such clarifying moments—an invitation to examine the root and fruit of who we are beneath our delusions, an invitation to "see what is really happening here." In short, an invitation to essay.

Toy Soldiers

I sit with Ian on the floor in our basement, wooden blocks and green army men lying all around us, and a scattering of other toy creatures mixed in for good measure—a platoon of Lego men, a menagerie of plastic dinosaurs, and a large stuffed giraffe slumped on the couch like some drunken god overseeing the battlefield. On his side of the room, Ian constructs a three-story fortress and mans every ledge and balcony with small, green, plastic soldiers: A lone private with a rifle on his shoulder, his weight shifted to one foot. A marksman on the move with his gun in both hands. A kneeling soldier with his rifle drawn to the hip. Another lying prone as he sights down the barrel of his carbine. A foot soldier hurling a grenade, his rough plastic features the picture of desperation. Out front, Ian has placed a single scout, leading the charge. The soldier carries only a pair of binoculars, and though he's clearly moving forward, he casts his eyes back at the other troops, and he's raised his right hand in a gesture that says something like "Let's get the bastards."

A no-man's-land stretch of carpet separates Ian's battalion from mine, and while he's ready for battle, I have not yet begun to build. I stare at my pile of blocks, a heap of motley army men collapsed all around me, and my imagination fails, or rather, it beats itself at its own game. My boys and I have been building block castles and bunkers to house our toy soldiers for years—but on this Sunday afternoon, I'm having trouble coaxing out my inner child. Maybe I've been watching too much of the news— too many images of bombed-out cities in faraway places, too many threats from hawkish politicians, too many news clips of schoolchildren running from gunfire—but somehow, the army men that Ian has set out in array seem all too eager for the fight, and in the middle of what is supposed to be a sleepy weekend diversion, I find myself wondering about the ethics of playing at war, of turning the chaos and violence of battle into a game with my sons, of celebrating the tools that make killing one another these days seem so easy, so efficient, and so fun.

I think I had what amounts to a fairly typical American boyhood— which is to say, I learned at a very young age to carry around masculinity and mayhem in the same psychological box. In my neighborhood every boy had his own arsenal of toy weapons— minilugers and lever-action rifles, plastic Uzis and cap-gun revolvers, shotguns that fired rubber darts, and even AK-47s with faux-woodgrain stocks. I've got a photo from the mideighties that captures my brother Josh at his ninth or tenth birthday party; in it he's wearing a green plastic helmet marked with a white star, and he's lifted a replica M16 to his shoulder—the kind with a built-in tension mechanism that made a rat-a-tat-tat sound when he pulled the trigger. The military industrial toy complex was thriving in the 1980s, and we all bought into it.

On Saturday afternoons we divided into teams and scattered out across the suburban battlefield to wage an ongoing war of onomatopoeic gunfire and strict rules of engagement. You could shoot through a tree limb, but parked cars were bulletproof, and if you got shot, it took the count of thirty Mississippis before you could rejoin the battle. When we couldn't play war outside, we watched *G. I. Joe* on television or played with our G. I. Joe army men on the living room carpet and imagined ourselves as members of some elite special forces unit saving the world from fascism. Most of us weren't old enough to see *Rambo* or *Platoon* or *Full Metal Jacket*, but we had older brothers who reenacted all the bloody bits for us in gruesome detail; on the news we had Central American rebel fighters, tanks rolling through Tiananmen Square, and all manner of Cold War posturing. We simply played at what we saw. I remember the electric feel of a toy gun in my hand, and how easy it was to see myself fighting on the front lines, creeping through the jungle, mowing down bad guys and screaming, "Die Commie!" at the top of my lungs. *Natural* might be the best word for it—an intuitive sense that a part of me was designed for violence.

Evolutionary psychologists have a theory about the origins of such aggression. The male warrior hypothesis, it's called, and it goes something like this: men have been in competition with each other for so long that we've developed a psychological predisposition to form tribes, stake out boundaries, and protect our turf (turf, in this case, being the ladies, as well as the resources that make us wealthy enough to attract those ladies). In other words, for our deep human ancestors, success was intimately connected to power, and power came by muscling out the competition, controlling resources, and attracting mates. If you had the power, you were more likely to make babies, and those babies in turn were more likely to grow up and repeat the cycle. Survival of the fittest, in this case, meant survival of the most aggressive, and for all we learn from the world around us, it may be that we are hardwired for violence from the beginning.

Consider my oldest son, Callan, at eighteen months, sitting in his highchair eating a piece of toast. At that age, he had never, to our knowledge, witnessed gunplay of any kind on TV or otherwise; he'd never held or even seen a toy gun; his rapidly developing gray matter should have been completely firearm free. And yet, there he was, sitting in his highchair wielding an L-shaped piece of toast like a pistol. He'd been chewing on one corner of that toast when something about the emerging shape caught his attention, seemed to remind him of something. Then he pointed his makeshift weapon at Melissa and said, "Pew, pew; pew, pew," and smiled wide liked he'd just discovered some grand secret about himself.

Callan's little brothers arrived to our family with basically the same inclinations, and as both Nolan and Ian got old enough, they too began making weapons out of nearly everything—sticks from outside, silverware, the can opener in our kitchen, empty toilet paper rolls; if something even vaguely resembles a firearm, they've probably pointed it at each other and pretended to shoot. Today we have an entire closet under our stairs dedicated to Nerf guns, plastic swords, and a bow with foam-tipped arrows. We call it the armory, and sometimes on a Saturday I'll walk by and find Ian and one of his little friends outfitting themselves for combat. Rifles slung over their shoulders and pistols tucked into their waistbands, bandanas tied around their heads and maybe a bicycle helmet strapped on tight. By now they've all played so many hours of shoot-'em-up video games and seen so much gunplay on TV that it's impossible to separate what they've learned from what might be instinct, but watching them suit up and march off to an imaginary war in the backyard, I find it fairly easy to imagine that they were born for this sort of thing.

And yet, I resist the male warrior hypothesis and the way it privileges the fight response over flight—hasn't human survival depended on the concerted application of both instincts? Knowing when to avoid conflict is at least as important as knowing when to embrace it. But in the world of video games and action movies, there's no such thing as a hero who succeeds by talking things out. It's *Duke Nukem*, not "duke negotiate with 'em." And I also worry about the oversimplification of masculinity in general, that reducing all men to spear-toting grunts programmed for nothing more than violence and sex might do as much to excuse all manner of bad behavior as explain it. And bad behavior aside, what if I'm just terrible with a spear? Or at getting the girl? In a system where the only true male is the alpha male, the rest are condemned to either accept their place in the hierarchy or find some way to jump the line. And in such a system, what other choice do beta boys have but violence?

Still, there's something deeply sentimental about the simple model of the heroic male warrior—the stoic, self-sacrificing soldier of the Hollywood war movies I watched with my dad as a kid. He loved a good war movie, and from the time I was little, I'd sidle up on the couch whenever he had one running—*Bridge on the River Kwai, Tora! Tora! Tora!, The Great Escape*. I probably saw *Empire of the Sun* a dozen times before graduating from high school, and it seemed as if Dad watched *Memphis Belle* once a month. The 1990 trailer for *Memphis Belle* shows a band of young airmen on a series of World War II bombing runs, and the entire premise of the movie is captured in a pithy voice-over: "We asked these boys to become men . . . we asked these men to become heroes . . . but whatever the danger, whatever the odds, we asked them to come home." Most everything Dad watched dripped with this same bellicose, reductive version of patriotic masculinity. He'd grown up in the shadow of the Greatest Generation, eating up war stories about his uncle, a decorated bomber pilot, and imagining himself into the gun-smoke battles of every John Wayne or Clint Eastwood film he could get tickets to. He joined the navy at seventeen, spent four or five years traveling around the world on Uncle Sam's dime and got out only because he wanted to go to college.

He once told me that leaving the military was a huge mistake. "I thrived on the structure," he said, but I think he also thrived on the automatic social status that attended a man in uniform. The military gave him an identity, some confidence, and a purpose; taught him his first trade; and helped him mature into adulthood. And yet, I remember around age twelve digging through his closet one afternoon and coming across his navy "Crackerjack" jumper—a dark-blue uniform for enlisted men that he wore on leaves and at formal occasions. The uniform was made of thick, rough wool and was small enough that at first I couldn't imagine my dad ever fitting into it, even at seventeen. The jumper looked more like a Halloween costume than a soldier's uniform; less the wardrobe of a man and more the getup of a boy heading out to play.

How long have little boys been playing at war? Probably for as long as their fathers have been marching off to fight. Who knows, but some prehistoric nomad carved a limestone male protector to accompany the famous Venus of Willendorf—a spear-wielding warrior to keep hostile tribes at bay—a Mars of Willendorf, if you will. A thousand years ago, Viking children played with toy boats carved from wood, and I can imagine a group of them conjuring up a raiding party in their minds, making landfall with their little vessels on the shore of some made-up country to the south where they'd sack invisible cities and raid make-believe villages. I can picture the sons of Japanese Bushido prowling their home gardens with sticks at their waists, drawing out their fake swords to cut off the heads of unsuspecting flowers. In thirteenth-century Germany, the children of the wealthy played with armies of tiny lead soldiers produced by boutique toy makers. These boys waged ground-shaking battles on the parlor room floor while the men in their lives were out leading actual soldiers into battle, and though they did not know it then, they were establishing Europe's first market for mass-produced toy soldiers.

At first, manufacturing costs kept the toy soldier market small— only the children of the wealthiest could afford little armies. But by the end of the nineteenth century, cheap tin soldiers were everywhere, and the playroom of your average rosy-cheeked young boy might easily be stocked with soldiers from around the world— warriors of ancient Egypt, marines of Napoleonic France, and rifle-bearing redcoats from Her Majesty's Royal Army.

The historian Kenneth Brown estimates that in 1901 the British market for toy soldiers was two and a half million boys strong, not counting the many thousands of adults who collected the toys, and even played with them. Well-known politicians and writers, including Winston Churchill, G. K. Chesterton, Robert Louis Stevenson, and H. G. Wells, engaged in war games in their own parlors and gardens. Wells went so far as to write a how-to book called *Little Wars* that laid out elaborate rules for his particular brand of domestic warfare. Even senior military officers took up the hobby and encouraged their junior officers to as well, believing war games could help military leaders develop their strategic capabilities. In the twenty years leading up to World War I, toy soldier manufacturers sprang up all over London, and by 1910 the most successful firms were producing eight hundred thousand soldiers a month.

According to Brown, when it came to the British psyche, toy soldiers were not merely playthings. Rather, those millions of tiny army men were part of a "complex web of educative influences, both formal and informal, which linked the games of the nursery floor to the adolescent and adult worlds." In other words, British boys learned the mythic glamorization of war as they played out elaborate battles with their toy soldiers at home. Later, the Boy

Scouts, the Boys' Brigade, and other youth organizations helped carry the myth of the British warrior into adolescence. By the time many young men were old enough to volunteer for the army, soldiering, battle tactics, and heroic notions of victory were all wrapped up in thoughts of home, and all a man needed was a bit of a patriotic push. When World War I erupted in 1914, the British government put out the call: "Your King and Country Need You: Join the Army until the War Is Over." In the first two months of the conflict, seven hundred thousand British soldiers enlisted, many of them original members of the first mass market for toy soldiers—young men for whom the notion of soldiering may have been deeply intertwined with their notions of patriotism, competitiveness, sportsmanship, masculinity, and nostalgia.

Brown quotes Charles Edmunds from his memoirs of the war in which he describes feeling caught between fear and excitement as he received his first battle orders. "Attacks I was familiar with, but they were attacks over known ground against imaginary enemies. Fighting I knew, but it was fighting dream battles with visionary foes." Later, in his description of jumping into a trench as a mortar exploded nearby, Edmunds captures the strange relationship between soldiering and child's play. "I was no more afraid than if it were a game. . . . This was as good fun as playing soldiers in the garden at home."

German princes in high-walled castles, British lads in London parlors, my own boys in our low-ceiling basement—centuries of deeply engrained cultural education as much a part of life as breakfast or swing sets or postgame snacks at peewee soccer. But for as many hours as my boys have logged playing soldiers on the carpet, today, more often than not, their soldiers of choice are digital, their battlefields as expansive as the online worlds they inhabit, and the effect on their collective psyches feels so far out of my control it leaves my head spinning. Sure, we have fairly strict rules about screen time, but they still manage a few hours a week shooting it out with some friends (or, more often, some strangers) on the other end of an internet connection.

They like to play a cartoonish, third-person shooter game that involves parachuting onto a small island where they scavenge for weapons and engage in a free-for-all battle to the death with a hundred other online players. Their avatars have exaggerated features, brightly colored hair, and zany action-figure costumes that create a game experience with a friendly, comic-book feel, but the ultimate objective of the game is simple: stay alive and kill as many of your opponents as possible. They start each round with a pickax for breaking down objects and collecting building materials, but by rifling through attics and basements and closets throughout the island, they can acquire a vast cache of weapons, everything from simple handguns and rifles to shoulder-fired rocket launchers and high-powered assault weapons. Better than that: kill another player and you can loot all their weapons and supplies for yourself.

When my boys aren't launching grenades or rattling off rounds of ammunition into the wooden walls of an abandoned barn, they're scouring the landscape for enemies, flushing them out into the open, zooming in with their scopes, and picking one another off. They kill with the long-distance accuracy of a sniper and the point-blank brutality of an assassin. They talk about in-game achievements and rewards for everything from headshots to body counts, and when they're not playing, they want to watch YouTube videos of the experts—guys who make a living playing video games while other people watch. At the dinner table we've had to make a rule against reliving digital battlefield moments alongside conversations about school and homework and Little League.

That pleasure of reliving each kill is maybe the thing that perplexes me most. My boys can record gameplay and save clips to share with their friends or upload them to YouTube. They can watch twenty-minute video compilations online with titles such as "Kills of the Week," "Savage Snipes," and "Top 50 Epic Kills and Funny Moments." Even after hours of green army man warfare, my boys had never wanted to relive even the most brutal acts of destruction they imagined on the battlefields of our living room. Real-world play seems to have less of the performative in it than their play in the digital world. If there was any kind of posturing on the living room floor, it manifested in a competition of imaginations.

"My plane swoops in and drops bombs on your castle," one boy might say.

"Well my sharpshooters blast your bombs out of the sky," says the other.

"And when they explode, shrapnel falls all over your men."

"But all my men are wearing shrapnel-proof helmets!"

The on-screen experience may seem more intimate—they're actually pulling triggers on their controllers and watching enemies fall—but video-game war play involves all the imaginative energy of shooting digital fish in a barrel. If a toy soldier battle risks reducing the horrors of war to a Sunday afternoon diversion, at least it taxes my boys' creative faculties to imagine the fates of the dozens or hundreds of little army men at their disposal. Sure, on the screen they can move and build and hide, but the nature of the video game effectively reduces them to the weapons in their avatars' hands, and the only significant choice they face is when to shoot.

Despite all that, my boys would argue that the game is pretty clean—there's no blood, no real carnage, and when they're not shooting at each other, they can dance or mug for the camera the way a wide receiver might after scoring a touchdown on national television—their avatars can break-dance, moonwalk, dab, or even do some hula—gestures that add a certain silliness to the game and tend to lighten an in-world mood that might otherwise be bogged down by all that slaughter.

Not that they ultimately want a lighter mood—particularly when it comes to Callan. He's always talking about the gorier games his friends play, always testing the waters to see if we might budge on the latest M-rated, first-person shooter—spy thrillers, lifelike war simulators, and one-man-against-the-universe alien bloodbaths. But he's always been our kid with the most interest in military culture and the sanguinary fun of gunplay. He's read nearly every Clive Cussler and Tom Clancy novel available at the local library, dozens of books on military strategy, histories of weaponry and warfare, and even a few books on espionage and codebreaking.

He subscribes to a YouTube channel run by a firearm enthusiast who lives out on a ranch in Texas and publishes good-ol'-boy demonstration videos with titles such as "Does Phone Book Body Armor Work?," "Firing a Pistol Submerged in Gasoline," "I Shot My Truck with a Tank," and "Bullet Proof Groin." Every few months Callan tells me how much he wants to go shooting, and recently, in brainstorming for a science fair project, he and his friends made several unsuccessful proposals for experiments involving weapons. When the teacher pointed out the zero-tolerance policy for such projects, they came up with a work-around—they designed and built their own bullet-proof riot shield using baking sheets, roof shingles, and a panel of plexiglass. He's not an overly aggressive kid, but he has talked fondly about what he imagines is the satisfying release of blowing things up.

I know he's drawn to the power of firearms, but he's also fascinated by the science and engineering involved, so I guess I can't begrudge him his hobby completely, but I still cringe a bit at the game he makes of the very serious matter of war and death. Especially when I think of the news and the relentless parade of men with guns—men driven mad with resentment, anger, fear, and hate; men in search of power, control, attention, and revenge; men who see deliverance in the hard, gleaming barrel of a semiautomatic rifle. It's hardly fair to conflate gun enthusiasm with the insanity of a mass shooting, but watching my boys watch their favorite YouTube personality laugh as he demonstrates the armor-piercing, organ-obliterating force of his latest outsized, military-grade rifle acquisition, I get squeamish at the cavalier celebration of weapons designed to mow down men by the dozens. Not to mention the implication that the right gun can be a shortcut to manhood. In the darkest corners of my parenting imagination, it is easy to see all this as some kind of slippery slope, to make the leap—however far it may be—from assault rifle as outlet for patriotic entertainment and masculine catharsis to assault rifle as the ultimate compensatory fantasy in the face of impossible expectations imposed by toxic male culture. All men know the emasculating pangs of rejection and failure, but something in our world is telling a heartbreaking number of us that when life backs you into a corner, an appropriate response is to shoot your way out.

In a conversation about male aggression and how the wider world is affecting my children, video games and spy novels and the glamorization of assault rifles seem like too easy a target, so to speak. Sure, my sons and I may have some deep evolutionary predisposition to aggression that's wrapped up in the biological imperatives to promulgate the species, and there may be some consequences of feeding that disposition with violent video games, YouTube displays of gratuitous Second Amendment worship, and a closet full of Nerf guns, but there's a bigger influence that trumps all of that—me. What are the consequences for my boys of being a witness to my own dark days? What do they internalize by watching me stomp through the kitchen, or slam a door, or use my booming Dad voice to stop them short in the middle of some back-and-forth bickering, or worse, when my patience dries up completely and I throw my weight around to solve a problem? I gave up spanking a long time ago, almost as soon as I tried it out, but I have been guilty of being too rough with my boys, of taking them by the arm, of holding them still while I get my point across, of using fear as a parenting tool. I find myself wanting to describe all this as the routine violence of family life, as if to excuse it as something inevitable about fathers and sons (another word for it, after all, is "manhandling"), but of course there shouldn't be anything inevitable or routine about it. For all my angst about their fascination with gunslinging in video games and on YouTube, the research is fairly split about any long-term negative effect of consuming violent media. On the other hand, there's almost complete consensus about the negative effects of aggression in the home.

And even when throwing my weight around is not about discipline but about horseplay, I know there's a fine line between helping my boys learn something about their physical boundaries and simply teaching them a lesson. Since they were little, I've tossed them in the air, swung them from my arms, carried them on my back, and grappled with them on the floor. As soon as my oldest was big enough, we started playing a game called "King of the Couch," where I lay on the sofa and he did everything but kick or punch or pinch to get me on the floor, and as Nolan and Ian got older, it became a three-on-one brawl that almost always ended with me on the carpet, battered and stretched, and three boys sitting gleefully on the couch, looking over their new dominion. Sure, psychologists say this kind of play is important for helping them test their limits and develop some confidence, especially when I let them win a little. But in the process, I know that recognizing a limit can also breed resentment. I've seen this in each of them, but particularly in my younger boys—Nolan and Ian. When a little wrestling or horseplay turns into something else—when what's meant to be a tap becomes a smack, or someone gets pinned down a little too long, or their pride gets hurt—they transform ever so briefly into something animal, or perhaps oedipal, and a part of them wants me dead. I've seen it play out in their own roughhousing, when getting hit too hard by a brother turns into retaliation and then a full-blown grudge match that requires Dad to step in and break things up. Tumbling around the living room with me and with each other has taught them all about boundaries, but it may also have been their first lesson on the male pecking order, and it may have taught them early to hate the bottom.

If aggression has its roots in a primal need for power and control, then there may be few things more aggravating than raising children. After all, despite the best efforts of parents, children will make their own choices, will often fail to live up to expectations, will see the world differently, and will likely be oblivious to the efforts their parents make for them. Mostly, they will be thirsty for their own sense of autonomy. I'm intimately familiar with how a kid's need for independence can push a parent toward the edge of emotional control. I've experienced the frustration of telling a kid that he can't wear a dirty shirt to school for a third day in a row. I know what it is like to hear a kid whine about a meal that I've just spent an hour cooking, to enter a room I've just cleaned and find it covered in toys, or to get a phone call from school that my son has punched someone on the playground. I've had pointless debates about who started a sibling scuffle or who made the mess in the bathroom or who broke the toy or who snuck the last cookie. I've tried to reason with an angry teenager who doesn't understand the purpose of his curfew or the purpose of completing his homework or the purpose of speaking kindly to his little brothers. I've hounded boys all morning about cleaning up their rooms and raised my voice at a boy for raising his voice at his mother. And there's no reason any single one of these minor conflicts should set a parent off, but the nature of parenting is that such conflicts pile up and pile on, and for all but the most emotionally balanced among us, what might on any other day be just another irritation can make us explode in an instant. The tension between parents and children is as primal as anything, and it is one reason the landscape of a home can so often feel like a battlefield.

My own father wasn't much into horseplay, but he did have a temper, and though it softened significantly over the years, I have more than a few memories of hiding around a corner while he and my older brothers fought. Usually they just yelled, but occasionally their disagreements would get physical—one of my brothers taking a swing at him or pushing him away or Dad wrestling one of them to the ground or pinning one in a head-lock. I don't remember that Dad ever started these fights, but he wasn't above defending himself, and if my brothers share some blame for throwing a first punch or two, then Dad shares some blame for letting arguments get that far out of control in the first place. I was too little to do much more than stay out of the way and feel bad that everyone was so angry all the time, but there was one thing that seemed clear to me, even then—keeping the peace was a dad's job. And mine wasn't very good at it. But the resentment I've harbored over the years has more or less subsided, largely because I let go of the expectation that my father should have been perfect and learned a bit more about the battlefield of his own childhood.

This is the short version: Before Dad was even born, his father ran off to join the army. When Dad was just a toddler, his mother suffered a mental breakdown and dumped him and his two brothers at Grandma's house for a few years. He spent the next decade bouncing around from one relative to another, sometimes living with grandparents or an aunt, other times living with his mother and her new husband, Roy. If any of the fight or flight response is learned, then the adults in Dad's life taught him the extremes of both. When his mother wasn't out late drinking away the pressures of parenting, she was at home responding to those pressures with an open palm. Dad would get hit for expressing his opinion or for not expressing it quickly enough. If he broke a rule, he'd get beat for lying about it. If he confessed, he'd get beat for telling the truth. When she dropped him at a relative's house, he'd get an earful about what a burden he was, and when she finally picked him back up, she'd tell him almost daily how having kids had ruined her life. "There was no negotiating anything at home," Dad tells me. "I got slapped around and yelled at, and that's how I learned to handle my own business." He hardly went a day at school without getting into some playground scuffle, and when he could no longer take all the fighting, he decided to escape. Joining the navy was as much an act of survival as anything else.

It really is no wonder that Dad locked horns with my brothers so often. For all the larger-than-life heroes he admired on the movie screen, he had virtually no real-life heroes in his own family. No models for how to arrive at that space between fight and flight where healthy conflict takes place. Instead, the trajectory of his parenting approach has been a gradual swing from one survival mechanism to another. With my older siblings it meant shouting matches and strong-arm authoritarianism, but by the time I was old enough to fight with him, he seemed less interested in confrontation. If I yelled or railed against him for some perceived failure or offense, he nearly always took it in stride, let me air out my grievances, and then he'd tell me he was sorry. In those moments of conflict, I felt a wild will to fight, a desperate need to prove something, to stand my ground as a matter of principle, but Dad wouldn't engage, and for years I failed to see this restraint as the personal accomplishment that it must have been. After decades of choosing to fight, by the time he'd come around to me Dad had learned the value of retreat.

Playing army with my boys in the basement, watching them shoot each other on the sprawling battlefield of some online game, or looking over their shoulders as they absorb the impulsive id of YouTube gun culture, I'm admittedly uncomfortable with how casual they seem about playing with death. And knowing how closely they watch me every day, I'm even more uncomfortable with how they're taking real-world cues from me about anger, aggression, and violence. And yet for as much as I played guns as a kid, for as natural and energizing as it felt, today I'm basically a pacifist. I don't own a single firearm, have no desire to shoot one, and I harbor all the typical skepticism about military culture and traditional patriotism that you might expect from a liberal academic. As for the anger and violence I witnessed as a kid, I've largely been able to avoid that in my own home. Dad improved on his past; I'm improving on mine, and what's to say my boys won't improve on theirs? And what's to say that, in the end, I or their environment will have much to do with that improvement anyway? Think of Callan with that toast in his highchair or Nolan and Ian giving me death-stares during a supposedly friendly wrestling match. They may carry inside them more ingredients for their future than the outside world could ever contribute. Yes, they're sponges, and they're going to get excited about guns and explosions and warfare in all the ways the world encourages them to, and they can't help but learn good and bad from my own example, but they're also the products of complex genetic evolution and individual personality, and perhaps I'm wasting my energy worrying about the fleeting interests of little boys playing at war the way little boys have done for millennia.

Recently, I looked up that H. G. Wells book, *Little Wars*, to see exactly how turn-of-the-century parlor battles in Great Britain compared to the battles that I've waged with my boys in our basement, and I was surprised by the similarities. Wells describes elaborate battlefields fortified by wooden block structures and populated by legions of small toy troops; he describes facing off with his sons or occasionally another grown man that he can persuade to join him on the floor. The book also includes an elaborate set of rules that Wells and his sons developed to make an actual competition out of their carpet skirmishes. What strikes me though is that unlike some of the military leaders of his day, Wells saw his *Little Wars* not as a training ground to make men better at actual war, but as a cathartic exercise that just might help keep the world at peace. "How much better is this amiable miniature than the Real Thing!" writes Wells. "Here is a homeopathic remedy for the imaginative strategist. Here is the premeditation, the thrill, the strain of accumulating victory or disaster—and no smashed nor sanguinary bodies, no shattered fine buildings nor devastated country sides, no petty cruelties, none of that awful universal boredom and embitterment, that tiresome delay or stoppage or embarrassment of every gracious, bold, sweet, and charming thing that we who are old enough to remember a real modern war know to be the reality of belligerence."

It's Wells's experience-based wariness that I appreciate most. He's seen the horrors of war and seems to understand the dangers of celebrating it without reservation. But he also seems to point out the need for a way to channel those baser instincts; while he finds pleasure in the game of war, he's got no delusions about its realities. This is the kind of thoughtfulness that I want to cultivate in myself even as I enjoy a good war movie, a thoughtfulness I hope lies dormant in my boys even as they blast away at digital enemies on the computer screen, a thoughtfulness that will eventually help them see armed conflict with a little sobriety, masculinity with a little nuance. Once again, from H. G. Wells: "All of us in every country, except a few dull-witted, energetic bores, want to see the manhood of the world at something better than aping the little lead toys our children buy in boxes. We want fine things made for mankind—splendid cities, open ways, more knowledge and power, and more and more and more."

The truth is, each of us carries around a deeply nuanced core, and it contains this *more* that Wells pines for, but we have to seek it out ourselves. For my boys and me, there is a *more* to manliness—more than guns and bulging muscle. There is a *more* to war—more than the spectacle of heavy weaponry and dazzling explosions. For all of us, there is a *more* to ourselves—more than the myopic expectations of Hollywood, more than the poor examples of our past, more nuance, more skepticism, more compassion, less hyperbole. There is a *more* to all of this, and all of us, if we but cultivate the imagination to find it.

Imagine, for instance, if my boys opened a new pack of little green army men, and along with the grenade-throwing captain, the brave scout, the determined rifleman, and that obedient private there were also shell-shocked troops curled in the fetal position, soldiers laid up in hospital beds nursing amputations, maybe a soldier back home waiting on the phone with the VA, one in civilian clothes trying to find work and struggling to relate with his family, one contemplating a bottle of pills or the end of his rifle. What if there were a collection of civilians—small plastic children cowering beneath their school desks during an air raid; a young child soldier struggling to hold the weight of his AK-47; a startled wedding party in the desert, casting their eyes toward the sound of a passing drone; a self-satisfied academic holding his nose up at American gun culture; or small plastic oligarchs and arms dealers, fat and happy, stuffing their pockets with little plastic wads of cash?

What if, along with the glories of war, their toys taught them something of its consequences? I don't pretend to think that we have no need of a military—I've learned enough of evil around the world to know the value of brave soldiers—but when I think about those soldiers, and the soldiers they head off to fight, it's hard not to think of them all as the children they once were; it's hard not to feel like Wells: "Great War is at present, I am convinced, not only the most expensive game in the universe, but it is a game out of all proportion. Not only are the masses of men and material and suffering and inconvenience too monstrously big for reason, but—the available heads we have for it, are too small."

At present the collective imagination of nations and peoples still puts too much stock in sending young folks off to play soldier every few years, and when I think about the long history of this madness—about the lives and treasure we dedicate to walling off our lands and building forts and aiming our turrets toward the coast, when I think about the endless stream of guns and soldiers that roll off assembly lines every day, when I think about fighter jets posturing in disputed airspace or tired soldiers amassed along barbed-wired borders or smoldering neighborhoods pocked by gunfire and mortar blast, when I think about my boys reveling over the new toy guns they got for Christmas or bragging about the "sick kills" they've racked up online—I can't help but wonder what we all might get up to as a human family if we weren't so busy trying to blow one another into oblivion? I can't help but wonder where our imaginations might take us if we didn't occupy them so often with fantasies of our own destruction?

Just the other day, Melissa and I went out to dinner and left the boys home with free reign to get on the Xbox and kill as many aliens and avatars as their little hearts desired, which is what we figured they would do. But when we got home, we found all three of them huddled around the television, controllers in hand, playing a game entirely devoted to building things—it's basically a virtual Lego set, and while you can occasionally kill giant spiders and green monsters or even slay a dragon, by and large the game is about exploration, creation, and cooperation. They build in an endless digital world with seemingly infinite possibilities: they can work online by accessing massive servers where sometimes hundreds of players all over the planet are working away, building and sharing space and admiring each other's work. There are solo builders that have spent unimaginable hours creating virtual models of entire cities—Paris, Manhattan, St. Louis—and there are build teams that work collectively to bring sprawling fantasy worlds to virtual life.

Our boys had spent the evening constructing houses and castles and underground tunnels and exploring the seafloor and helping each other on their projects. That image, even though it be a rare one, is something I can hold on to—the three of them building something together, playing at a make-believe world where you might raise a barn, dig a swimming pool, plant a garden, or frame a house. A world where the water runs clean, and the ground offers up its abundance to anyone willing to dig, and blue skies sing overhead, the promise of an endless horizon glowing in the distance. And I know by holding that image in my mind, I'm just playing at a different fantasy; I know the world is an uglier, more dangerous, more complicated, less hospitable place than the virtual world my boys had run off to that night, but I also know the powerful effect of imagination, and perhaps the more we play at such worlds, the more inclined we all may be to fashion our real one after that kind of fantasy, for a change.

Girl Fight

Marty Manzoni's mother was fat. We all knew it, and we all knew better than to ever mention it, but that day in the school hall before basketball practice we were waiting for Coach to show up, and we got to talking about girls, as boys do, and someone mentioned Heather, a girl with sandy blond hair who carried her bulk around on ballerina tiptoes and who had told me just the day before, above the noise of the bus, that she liked me—a girl with whom, against my better sixth-grade judgment, I had secretly agreed to "go out."

Marty Manzoni, whose mother we all knew was fat, had been bouncing a ball in the hallway when he turned to me, smiling.

"Heather's a fat girl," he said. "Why do you like a fat girl?" And the boys around us laughed because my secret had gotten out that day, as secrets do, and they had all been wondering the same thing.

I might have said that Heather and I rode the same bus for years, that we both liked football and sang along with Boyz II Men, that we shared the kind of easy, endless conversations that later in my life I would recognize as the first signs of a good, healthy crush. I could have said I liked the idea of a girl liking me, and I could have said that he was ruining it all with his questions.

Instead, I chased him, as he must have known I would. I chased him down the hall and out the school's large double doors.

I chased him for Heather and for my stupid, boyish pride. But mostly I chased him for the giggling boys around us who left me no other choice, for making clear what I'd already figured out: that I couldn't love a fat girl, that no one can love a fat girl.

Marty ran across the parking lot and onto the school's large, green lawn, finally stopping beneath the flagpole, basketball tucked under his arm. I stayed at the curb and watched him standing there, his chest heaving, and then I opened my mouth and said the only thing a sixth-grade boy could say in a moment like that. And before the words—"Not as fat as your mom!"—left my mouth, I knew that insult would hang in the air, as insults do, and make the other boys gasp and shudder as it slowly settled into the ground around us.

Marty stood by the flagpole. Our teammates spilled out of the double doors to watch, chuckling. I turned, still breathing hard myself, and rejoined the group as if nothing had happened at all, as if my girlfriend wasn't fat, and I hadn't just breached some sacred boys' club boundary. But Marty inched forward to the edge of the asphalt and lifted the basketball. It hit me on the ear so hard I fell to the ground, my head ringing, and I cried louder than I have ever cried anywhere. It was an indignant, fearful cry, a where-is-my-mother cry, and the boys around me backed away, as if afraid they might catch something.

Then Coach pulled up in his car and stepped out, looked at me sprawled and bawling on the concrete, and then at Marty who walked past us both, picked up his basketball, and disappeared into the school. The other boys followed Marty in a mute procession past my body, and Coach held the door open to follow behind them. "Get up," he said, in a voice that meant, "You're acting like a girl."

But I didn't get up. Instead, I lay on the ground, half hoping that Heather might drive past with her mom and see me on the ground, screech to a halt, jump out of the car, kneel at my side and take my head in her arms; and the other half of me was hoping that she would never come to school again, that I might die right there on the asphalt, and this story along with me.

Good Enough

It is indeed the necessary condition of every work of human art or science, small as well as great, to advance toward perfection by slow degrees.

—ROBERT LOWTH, *A Short Introduction to English Grammar*, 1762

1. "A Good Man Is Hard to Find"

The other day I stepped out of my office and bumped into a campus custodian walking down the hall. For the longest time he and I had been strangers working in the same building, but one morning we shared an elevator and some small talk and discovered we had a mutual acquaintance. Now, when our paths cross like this, we exchange pleasantries in the clunky manner of co-workers who might, given time, become friends.

"How are you?" I asked, stepping with him down the hall, and he said he was good, but then he corrected himself.

"Eh, I mean *I'm well*," he said and laughed. And I laughed with him, and we talked about the weekend and the weather, and then I stopped in at the faculty mailroom, and he continued down the hall.

Since then I've thought a lot about this brief moment of grammatical self-consciousness; when you teach writing for a living, everyone assumes you're a grammar Nazi, that you'll think less of them for their *ain't*s and *gonna*s, their anxious use of *anxious*, their misplaced *lay*s and loose-lipped *lie*s. But if they only knew the truth—that I still can't reliably explain why you're not supposed to end a sentence with a preposition, that I always have to look up the difference between *lay* and *lie*, and that I have no idea why "I'm well" is theoretically better than "I'm good"—they might not second-guess their language so often around me, might not feel the need to correct themselves all the time, and my custodian friend might not walk through the halls of the English Department wearing his own language like a millstone.

Then again, I'm only assuming that my custodian friend was embarrassed by his grammatical slip, but his self-correction might simply have been a matter of politeness, the way adults might watch their mouths around small children; or his comment may have been a begrudging acknowledgment of rules he otherwise happily disregards, the way my lead-foot brother slows down when he sees a cop and then speeds up again once he rounds the corner; certainly my friend was aware, as most of us are, that when we speak, what is heard depends a great deal on who is listening.

A few years ago, I attended a conference hosted by a small, energetic woman whose primary mode of communication involved gesticulating with a clipboard in her hand and thanking people by saying "well aren't you sweet." She seemed to orchestrate the entire conference from that clipboard, a feat that included scheduling and staffing three days of seminar sessions, three keynote addresses, and three catered lunches for more than four hundred people.

On the third day of the conference, during a break between panel sessions, I asked her where she was from, and when she said "Georgia," I was surprised because she didn't have much of a southern accent.

"I learned to tone it down in college," she said. "But it was worth it."

"What do you mean?" I asked her. "What was it worth?"

"Well," she said and then paused. "About ten IQ points."

We laughed, but at the time, I was living in Lubbock, Texas, and I knew exactly what she was talking about—the range of accents in that part of the country is impressive. From the deepest drawls to the slightest twangs, vowels uttered on the Llano Estacado swing loose and relaxed—like saddlebags over the rump of a lazy horse, like a Colt .45 slack-holstered at the hip, like a tight-rolled cigar balanced on the lips. At least that's how I heard it then—with the condescending ear of a boy who watched too many westerns while growing up in the oatmeal-accented suburbs of Portland, Oregon. So many conversations conjured clichéd Hollywood images of crusty cowboys and hayseed farmhands that I found myself thinking, on more than one occasion, *everyone sounds like a bunch of hicks*. Not among my proudest moments as a temporary Texan.

Getting to know people usually helped readjust my assumptions, but when it came to first impressions—lawyer or grocery clerk, pastor or professor—the lower the swing in a person's West Texas drawl, the harder those assumptions were to shake. Linguists call this accent bias, though that is too nice a phrase for the plain-spoken bigotry of the thing—the very definition of prejudice, one bitter fruit of that often misguided question of right and wrong language, and a consequence of who gets to decide what's good and what's not.

2. "Up to No Good"

The question of goodness is, of course, about much more than language, and when it comes to hypercritical inclinations, accent bias is perhaps the least of my worries. From the moment I wake up in the morning, I'm passing judgment on my lazy kids for not putting away their shoes; on my wife, Melissa, for not making her side of the bed; on the dog for being unable to think about anything but playing fetch. Step outside and I'm judging that neighbor with a front yard full of weeds but also that neighbor with the golf-course grass and well-trimmed roses. And what about that bro who just showed up to the office in an oversized pickup? What's he compensating for? Or what about that other guy who drives the beat-up Corolla with a backseat full of garbage? Food stains on the face of some neighbor boy who comes over to play? Don't his parents notice? A preschool kid at church with perfectly gelled hair and a three-piece suit? That's borderline child abuse.

These are all actual thoughts I've briefly entertained in the past few months, and as fleeting as these unsavory judgments usually are, they recur, I think, because, like most of us, I'm looking for some concrete indication that my own life isn't a complete mess, and this kind of selective comparison makes it easy to think I'm doing alright (though my editor tells me that the correct phrase is *all right*). Unfortunately, such comparisons also reduce goodness to a checklist of social expectations, driven more often by marketing, nostalgia, insecurity, and ego than any internal moral compass. And the problem is I love checklists. I want goodness to be simple; give me a chart to fill out, a set of requirements to complete, a badge to earn. Please, gold stars, somebody. See how I pull a comb through my youngest son's hair on Sunday mornings and how I make sure his older brothers do the same? Check me out as I send them all off to school with washed faces and clean shirts; walk with me on my freshly mowed lawn, and notice the lines cut more or less on the diagonal; see the flower bed and how few weeds there are. Need a ride in my car? Don't worry, I've cleaned up the floor, or at least tossed everything in the trunk and brushed crumbs off the seat; and ask my wife, she'll tell you: I always make my side of the bed, and usually hers too. Aren't I good? Or, do I mean *well*?

3. *"The Good Old Days"*

Strange that language, as intrinsic as it seems, is ultimately a human construct; strange that at some point in the distant past, someone, or rather several someones, actually had to decide what meant what. Prescriptive notions of grammar have been around so long, helping us determine the difference between good and bad language, that it's hard to imagine a time when all those grade-school rules about spelling, punctuation, and grammar were ever up for discussion. And yet, if you and I could go back a few hundred years, we'd find ourselves in the middle of a raucous dispute about the vulgar, unruly nature of the English tongue. Okay, maybe not raucous, but certainly a dispute.

The most obvious issue? Spelling—no standard existed until the eighteenth century. For proof, behold the title of this 1586 pamphlet on the English language: "William Buollokar's abbreviation of hiz grammar of English extracted out-of hiz grammar at lar'g, for the spe'di parc'ing of English spe'ch and the aezier coming to the knowledg' of grammar for other languag'ez." And a deeper issue than spelling? Could English really have a grammar at all? Greek? Sure. Latin? *Certissime!* Those ancient and noble languages seemed, to scholars of the European Enlightenment, the very linguistic embodiment of reason and natural order. But English? As sixteenth-century pamphleteer James Howell wrote, "The English speech though it be rich, copious and significant . . . I cannot call it a regular language . . . there could never any grammar or exact syntaxes be made of it."

Nevertheless, hundreds of authors gave it a go. Between 1580 and 1800 the number of pamphlets, books, and articles published on the subject of English grammar doubled every few decades, from just one produced in the 1590s to more than fifty in the 1790s alone. At first these books were created to make Latin lessons easier, and in the process scholars fabricated all manner of artificial relationships between Latin and English grammatical structures—a move that gave birth to many groundless prohibitions in English. No double negative? No split infinitive? No preposition at the end of a sentence? You can blame all that on Latin. ——┼——

Soon though, scholars were studying English for its own sake, and seemingly everyone with a quill had an opinion on how one should speak and write, or at the very least were willing to take other people's opinions and repackage them as their own. There were grammar books for students and scholars, of course, but there were also self-help books for merchants, foreign travelers, and ambitious members of the working class who hoped that a bit of eloquence might help improve their social standing. Beyond that there were reams of gentlemanly commentary written for no other apparent reason than the pleasure of debate. Among my favorites is this sentence from the late eighteenth-century British thinker John Pinkerton, who expressed concern about the misuse of *S* in the English language, but not, apparently, about his type-setter's habit of using the symbol *f* with such abandon (see fig. 1) or about his own mispronunciation of the word *us* (also see fig. 1).

A N Y obſervation or diſcovery, which tends to the improvement of our lan-guage, gives me particular pleaſure : I there-fore agree with you in your applauſe of Mr. Sheridan's remark, that the S, which abounds ſo much in the Engliſh orthography, hath very often the power of Z. Why ſhould it not be written accordingly ? Why not ſpell *biz, uz, her'z ; enclozez, arizez,* &c. &c. &c.? I long to ſee that hiſſing letter as ſcarce in the language as poſſible.

FIG. 1. John Pinkerton on the misuse of *S* in the English language.

Amid this intellectual fervor Jonathan Swift wrote, "Our Language is extremely imperfect; that its daily Improvements are by no means in proportion to its daily Corruptions; and the Pretenders to polish and refine it, have chiefly multiplied Abuses and Absurdities; and, that in many Instances, it offends against every Part of Grammar." (Note that Swift evidently saw no corruption in the arbitrary insertion of capital letters.)

Today, when *Smithsonian* magazine claims that "Most of What You Think You Know about Grammar Is Wrong," or *Huffington Post* runs an article on "Why Only Some Grammar Rules Are Breakable," they're perpetuating arguments that got their start hundreds of years ago, but more than that, they're reminding us of the relationship between language and social propriety, that the words we use have a weight we can only partially know, and that in many situations, goodness is relative.

4. *"No Good Deed Goes Unpunished"*

In my home growing up I was the good kid, but the bar was pretty low. My older brothers and sisters had made careers out of suburban juvenile delinquency, skipping class, blowing off homework, sneaking out late—not to mention the occasional foray into shoplifting or dirty magazines. They raised a lot of hell for my parents, and I felt no small amount of pressure to compensate for all of them at one time or another—which may explain why I'm predisposed to the checklist approach to goodness. I went to church most every Sunday, stayed on the honor roll at school, earned my Eagle Scout badge, and dated a series of respectable girls whose parents were glad to see me pulling up in the driveway on a Friday night. I played sports, joined the drama club, hung out with kids from the speech and debate team, and always said hello to the special needs kids when we passed in the hall. Among the other students, I had such a reputation that they actually elected me Prince of Kindness during my senior year (I had a sash and everything), and I still remember the look of surprise on the face of a high school guidance counselor as she looked over my academic record during a college-prep interview. "You're a Franklin?" she asked, incredulous.

But the truth is, for all my "good" behavior, I was still a teenager, and something about being "good" left a sour taste in my mouth—like I might be missing out on some important aspect of juvenile self-actualization—as if quality of life could be measured by the quantity of risks one takes or the rules one disregards. But such was puberty, modern adolescence, and the privilege of suburban angst. And so in the midst of my college-prep marathon of commendable behavior, I tried on a little rebellion like a boy who tries on his older brother's smoky leather jacket or a girl who slips into her older sister's miniskirt—I humored that need to see a different version of myself in the mirror. What would I look like as an underachiever? As a rebel? As a kid who did whatever the hell he wanted to? As if to test this question, I skipped a bit of class, got my hands on the occasional dirty magazine, and made out with a few of those respectable girls I was taking out on Friday nights. And while these pedestrian risks helped appease a fear that I might be missing out on something, test-driving that devil-may-care attitude had the unintended consequence of making me feel, most of the time, like a complete hypocrite.

According to his memoir *This Boy's Life*, Tobias Wolff embraced teenage rebellion a lot easier than I ever did. He egged cars and stole from the local market; he smashed windows at his school, brawled with other boys, and routinely took late-night joyrides in the family car. Once he even got drunk and siphoned gasoline from a truck that belonged to one of the poorest families in the neighborhood. He was, by his own admission, less than exemplary, but he rarely thought of himself as "bad." He may have done bad things, but they were all circumstantial. Beneath his unruly behavior was a boy his mother would be proud of. Even when he applied to prep school using fake transcripts and forged reference letters filled with fictional accomplishments, Wolff felt he was simply "writing a truth known only to me." Sure he lied on his application, and while those lies were designed to cover up his less-than-stellar past, they were also intended to forecast his future; in essence, he described an aspirational version of himself: "I wrote without heat or hyperbole, in the words my teachers would have used if they had known me as I knew myself." Wolff recognized as a child that self-definition hinges on more than a simple enumeration of our deeds, that a discrepancy between what we believe and what we do is as much a sign of our humanity as a sign of any hypocrisy.

I'm pushing forty now, which means I should have all kinds of insight and maturity about oversimplified notions of goodness, but, as it is, the universe has blessed me with children, which is another way of saying the universe isn't done proving I'm a hypocrite. Raising three boys means I have ample opportunity to relive my own childhood mistakes and three reasons to fear history might repeat itself. Being a father means that instead of entertaining magnanimous, philosophical ruminations on goodness, I too often find myself wringing my hands over all the ways my boys might choose to be less than good. They've all committed the various misdemeanors of childhood—fighting in the basement, pestering each other to tears, claiming they've brushed their teeth when clearly they have not. And occasionally they've been guilty of worse—lying about where they're going, stealing money from each other, or picking on some kid at school. And even though all that is really not much more than I did as a child, on particularly trying days I can be overwhelmed by that unique version of irrational anxiety that only parents can fully appreciate—it's a snowballing apprehension that cuts a quick path from "You cheated on your homework?" to "You'll end up a forty-year-old alcoholic living in our basement." In the face of that anxiety, I am impatient for them to develop their own ethical backbones.

And impatience is really what it all comes down to. If parenting has taught me anything, it's that kids eventually figure things out. They learn to sleep through the night, to use the toilet, to eat without a bib, and they learn to say "thank you" and "sorry," and they learn to keep their hands off their brothers' piggy banks. And here's the kicker: my oldest has achieved all these benchmarks, as much in spite of me as because of me. Still, I'm impatient for the next benchmark, and the next one, and the one after that. *Hurry*, I want to say. *You've got to grow up.* Never mind that in my own stumbling process of "growing up," *time* has been, by far, the most important ingredient. And for all but the pathologically incapable among us, we grow out of our childhood quirks. We learn to own our messes and mistakes, we learn to share, to apologize, and to respect the property rights and personal space of others. And more than that, if we let it, time will teach us something about genuine goodness, will burden us with maladies both physical and mental, with cancers and broken bones and broken hearts, with depression and loneliness and sorrows and fears, and all these will make us targets for the kindness of others. Time will also provide us a friend, a partner, a parent, or, say, three impressionable sons to care for—human relationships as the ultimate incubators for our own burgeoning morality.

5. "As Good as Your Word"

One of the most popular English grammar texts to come out of the eighteenth century was Robert Lowth's *A Short Introduction to*

43

English Grammar, published in 1762. This little volume, written as a side project by a modest bishop in the Anglican Church, followed a pattern common for the time of breaking down English into its component parts—first letters, then syllables, and then words. But what made Lowth's book unique was the "sentences" section, which included a litany of errors by some of England's most beloved writers. He chastises Alexander Pope for dropping an *of* when he should have retained it, John Locke for insisting on a *whom* that should have been a *who*, and William Shakespeare for the sin of the double comparative in *The Tempest*, act 1, scene 1, when Prospero describes the daughter of the duke of Milan as "more braver." Not even the Bible, which he calls "the best standard of our language," finds refuge from Lowth's critique. The grammarian mentions at least twenty-three errors, taking particular issue with the Holy Writ's tendency to conflate the simple past form of a verb with its past participle form. Lowth allows that custom may account for some of these errors, but the rest are "wholly inexcusable." He points to the "absurdity" and perversion of these mistakes and calls the general use of phrases such as "I have wrote, I have drank [and] I have bore," as altogether "barbarous."

A Short Introduction to English Grammar proved wildly successful, with multiple editions printed in the 1760s and more than thirty-four thousand copies printed by 1780. Everyone from scholars and noblemen to merchants and students was taking Lowth's advice to heart, and the book would stay in regular circulation well into the nineteenth century. All of England, it seems, was eager for someone to lay down some concrete rules. Lowth's work was so popular that other scholars routinely borrowed from it, often without attribution, and a few lines of the text even made their way, verbatim, into a Charles Dickens novel. In her book *The Bishop's Grammar*, the linguist Ingrid Tieken-Boon van Ostade describes how language historians have long considered Lowth the epitome of the eighteenth-century prescriptivist—an arrogant, aristocratic bishop of London, bent on upholding certain high-class forms of speech, protecting Latinate influences, privileging stuffy formalities, and ignoring the vulgarities of common speech. She quotes the linguist Jean Aitchison who described Lowth as "pompous," "eccentric," "lamentable," and "pernicious," and points out that Bill Bryson once called Lowth's grammar "distressingly influential." To these critics, Lowth was, at best, a misguided pedant trying to foist conformity upon a language that preferred to live in the wild. At worst he was a despot grammarian trying to control the masses by way of linguistic authoritarianism. The truth, according to Tieken-Boon van Ostade (what a name!), is less nefarious: Lowth wrote the book for his son.

In a February 1762 letter to his friend, the poet James Merrick, Lowth explained: "I drew [my grammar] up for the use of my little Boy, for the reasons mentioned in the preface." And what does that preface mention? "It is with reason expected of every person of a liberal education, and it is indispensably required of every one who undertakes to inform or entertain the public, that he should be able to express himself with propriety and accuracy."

Far from despotic intentions, Lowth's simple goal was to help his son learn to speak well. Lowth himself was the son of a middle-class clergyman, which means he would have grown up in the linguistic borderlands of England, perhaps following his father into the homes of the very wealthy and the very poor, hearing conversations with both, noting the difference. I've just a spare knowledge of eighteenth-century Anglican liturgy, but I like to picture a young Robert Lowth swinging his feet beneath the adult-sized bench in church on Sunday, his father's familiar voice ringing off the high stone walls.

Remember not, Lord, our offences, nor the offences of our forefathers;
from all evil and mischief; from sin, from the crafts and assaults
of the devil; from thy wrath, and from everlasting damnation,
Good Lord, deliver us.

Around him in the front rows sit pedigreed men and women in fine clothing: the local aristocracy with their posh manners and ancient names, their polished shoes and ruffled sleeves—crisp and clean collars to go along with their crisp and clean language. And in the rows behind him, the peasantry in rough wool, their voices a bit louder, their manners full of mischief.

From all blindness of heart; from pride, vain-glory, and hypocrisy;
from envy, hatred, and malice, and all uncharitableness, Good
Lord, deliver us.

I imagine the casual energy of the working class attracting the young, fidgety child, but I also imagine he may have noticed more than once a sideways glance from some long-nosed lord sitting in the front row, or overheard a judgmental whisper or a vainglorious scoff. And above all, I imagine him listening, not just to his father's litany at service, but at home when his father entertained guests, on the road when his father stopped to comfort a beggar, when he visited the sick and dying.

From lightning and tempest; from plague, pestilence, and famine;
from battle and murder, and from sudden death . . . From hardness
of heart, and contempt of thy Word and Commandment, Good
Lord, deliver us.

I imagine young Robert at school, in the fields, and at the market, listening to street vendors and farmers, to soldiers and teachers, to stonecutters and coach drivers. I imagine him enthralled by the weight of the Word, but also by the weight of words, by the tension between a need for rules and the inevitability of variation. I imagine a young Robert Lowth caught between the propriety of those in the front pews and the personality of those in the back.

Whatever the origin of his linguistic preoccupations, Lowth grew into a man deeply concerned about language and its power in society. In the preface to his grammar's first edition, he describes his project as "An Essay, upon a Subject, tho' of little esteem, yet of no small importance." By the time he'd reached adulthood, he'd completed studies at Winchester and Oxford College; learned Hebrew, Latin, and Greek; tutored the son of a duke; toured Europe; and turned down a position as the bishop of Limerick. As a child, he would have seen firsthand how his father had leveraged linguistic skill into a successful career as a writer and preacher, and Lowth would have understood the importance of language in helping secure his own son's position in society. He doubtless understood that fair or not, doors opened and closed according, in part, to one's mastery of language, that every time we open our mouths, the world is taking note, passing judgment. Language may be a mystery, both arbitrary and beautiful, reliant upon the logic of a mathematical formula, and as spontaneous as lightning, but it can also bind like shackles.

6. "More Harm than Good"

I'm a God-fearing man, which means I subscribe to the biblical call to love my neighbor and turn the other cheek, and I read the Proverbs of Solomon with both fear and trembling: "Train up a child in the way he should go: and when he is old, he will not depart from it." My responsibility, at least according to Solomon, is pretty clear. And in some ways religion offers me and my boys a ready-made grammar of goodness, a dogma of dos and don'ts to keep us in line, but if training up a child were as simple as sending him off to church, we'd have fewer God-fearing men in prison right now. In the end, I think Solomon's counsel has as much to do with what my boys learn from me as with anything they might learn at Sunday school.

So I try and take the Good Samaritan approach (which is, incidentally, something I learned at Sunday school): stop on the side of the road when someone is stalled in a ditch; give rides to strangers; shovel snow for the old couple across the street; bake bread for the neighbors at Christmas. But my motives have always felt muddy. Is it good enough to do good because I hope my boys will learn something from it? I'm pretty sure true goodness probably means that your left hand really doesn't know, or at least doesn't care to point out what your right hand is doing. The strongest indication that I still have a long way to go is that every time my left hand doeth so much as pick up some litter on the street, my right hand wants to shoot up into the air and say, "Hey, boys, look at me. Over here. No big deal. Just saving the world, one piece of trash at a time."

What's wrong with hoping they pay attention to my best moments, when I know they're paying attention to my worst ones? As a parent, I find it easy to imagine I can hide my most unsavory faults from my kids. I put on my best face for work, and at home Melissa has more or less learned to live with all my quirks and shortcomings, but my children are quietly observing, taking notes, and one day they'll discover how often I fail to follow my own advice, and all the fatherly dos and don'ts I've been insisting on will become evidence for the prosecution when my kids inevitably put me on trial for being as human as they are.

Evidence for the prosecution: *You should have called. You should have been home earlier. You should have put away your shoes. You should have hung up your jacket. Get your housework done before you call your friend. Turn down your headphones. Don't watch that crap on television. Do you really need a screen in front of you all the time? Can't you play that with your little brother? No, you can't have a snack: dinner is in five minutes. Eat all your vegetables. Yes, even the mushrooms. Chew with your mouth closed. Your pants are not a napkin. Eat over your plate. If you're going to burp, cover your mouth. And say excuse me. No, you can't have ice cream on a school night. For the love—you could at least go in the other room if you're going to fart. Don't say fart. Don't say butt. Don't put your feet on the table. Shouldn't you be in bed? Don't walk away while I'm talking to you.*

The Old Testament repeats over and over again that God will "visit the iniquity of the fathers on the children to the third and fourth generation," which sounds harsh, unless you take into account the power of behavioral psychology. As one researcher put it, "Watching an adult doing something wrong can make it much harder for kids to do it right." Whatever generational curse lies at the heart of my boys' tantrums and moments of spite, I wonder how far back it goes; to what great-grandparent do we owe our various failures at goodness, and to what extent is it fair to blame them?

In Flannery O'Connor's famous short story "A Good Man Is Hard to Find," a homicidal maniac called the Misfit puts three bullets through the chest of an old woman pleading for her life. And it's a testament to O'Connor's depiction of this woman as a selfish schemer that her death doesn't seem entirely undeserved. From start to finish, the story depicts a grandmother who cares only about herself, who fails to admit when she is wrong, and who relies on passive-aggressive manipulation to get what she wants.

And what the end of the story offers, in vivid gothic horror, are the consequences of placing superficial metrics, such as good manners and social status, ahead of actual goodness. And the Misfit's famous line, "She would have been a good woman if it had been somebody there to shoot her every minute of her life," hangs there at the end of the story—an uncomfortable reminder that true goodness should not depend on circumstance. Perhaps the starkest consequence of the grandma's false goodness is the body count. Her inability to see the world from any perspective other than her own leads not only to her death, but the death of her son, her daughter-in-law, and her three grandchildren—false goodness wipes out three generations in one afternoon. O'Connor was never one for subtlety.

"Pure Religion," writes the apostle James, is "to visit the fatherless and widows in their affliction, and to keep himself unspotted from the world," and it's that last part that seems so hard: goodness with no worldly entanglements, no expectation of reward, no expectations at all; a boundless, organic goodness driven by imagination and empathy; a goodness that worries entirely about the widow in her affliction and not at all about checklists and social expectations; a willingness to do the right thing not because we hope to be seen by other people but because we've learned to truly see all people as they really are.

Here's a truth I'm still trying to grasp: stopping on the road to Jericho was not what made the Samaritan good, but rather it was his goodness that made him stop.

7. *"As Good as New"*

If you could gather the preoccupations of Lowth and his eighteenth-century fraternity of grammarians, throw them all into a large caldron, and boil them down to their essence, you'd find steaming at the bottom of that caldron one word: *propriety*. In his introduction, Lowth wrote that a grammar book should "teach us to express ourselves with propriety in that language." John Walker, who authored a widely used eighteenth-century pronunciation dictionary, hoped to "tempt the lover of their language to incline to the side of propriety." In Samuel Johnson's 1747 plan to write an English dictionary, he described his intention to "fix the English language" and "preserve the purity and ascertain the meaning of our English idiom." And all these men echo Defoe who, back in 1697, proposed the creation of a royal society "to encourage polite learning, to polish and refine the English tongue, and advance the so much neglected faculty of correct language, to establish purity and propriety of style, and to purge it from all the irregular additions that ignorance and affectation have introduced." And though Defoe never got his royal society, men such as Johnson, Lowth, and Walker were, in large measure, successful. The linguist Joan C. Beal refers to the trio as "the great triumvirate of eighteenth-century guides to usage," and Tieken-Boon van Ostade (say it again, you know you want to) writes that Johnson, Lowth, and Walker "were largely responsible for codifying the English language."

So, three cheers for our Georgian philologists for getting us all to agree on a standard usage and received pronunciation. But all this focus on arbitrary measures of propriety and purity, of top-down prescriptions for what is right and wrong, leaves me feeling uninspired and reminds me of Tobias Wolff again—but this time through the Anders character in his short story "Bullet in the Brain." Anders, a book critic known for his "weary, elegant savagery," finds himself in line at the bank during a robbery. Two armed men in ski masks come through the doors, subdue the security guard, and start ordering people around at gunpoint. "One of you tellers hits the alarm, you're all dead meat," says one of the masked men. Anders, who apparently can't control his inner critic, says out loud, "Oh, bravo. . . . Dead meat," and embarks on a running critique of the two masked men and their lame dialogue. His snickering at the bank robbers' clichés makes everyone around him nervous, and eventually one of the masked men approaches Anders, raises his pistol, and says, "You think I'm comical? You think I'm some kind of clown . . . f—— with me again and you're history. *Capeesh?*" At this point Anders, who can no longer contain his scorn, bursts out laughing, and the masked man shoots him in the head.

What flashes through Anders's mind (along with the bullet) is not the memory of his first love, not his wife and daughter, not any of the poetry he'd committed to memory or anything about his job as a book critic. What he remembers, instead, is a summer sandlot baseball game from his childhood, he and his friends choosing positions, and someone's cousin from out of town saying, "Shortstop. Short's the best position they is." Those last two words strike Anders deeply, and a realization about language opens up inside of him. He wants the boy to say it again, "but he knows better than to ask. The others will think he's being a jerk, ragging the kid for grammar. But that isn't it, not at all—it's that Anders is strangely roused, elated, by those final two words, their pure unexpectedness and their music."

This is an appreciation of language for what it is, not what it should be; a celebration of its "pure unexpectedness" over a demand for some artificial, platonic purity, an acceptance that language is as valuable observed in the wild as *etherized upon a table*, that any notion of "standard" language is, at best, subjective, and that everything from the stiffest British accent to the twangiest of Texas drawls is its own kind of standard.

It recalls a mindset that has driven an explosion of thought on language over the past hundred years. In the early twentieth century, the philosopher Ludwig Wittgenstein writes in *Philosophical Investigations*, "Philosophy may in no way interfere with the actual use of language; it can in the end only describe it." Around the same time, Ferdinand de Saussure gives us semiotics and the notion that language is wholly arbitrary, and that meaning shifts and mutates according to context. A similar idea shows up in Roland Barthes and his proclamation that the author is dead—that "every text is eternally written here and now" by whoever is reading it. In the 1960s Jacques Derrida develops his ideas of language as a slippery human construct that necessarily mediates our reality: "We are dispossessed of the longed-for presence [or, reality] in the gesture of language by which we attempt to seize it." More recently, thinkers such as Noam Chomsky and Steven Pinker have used neurology, psychology, and mathematics to wrestle with ideas about the evolution of language and its relationship to deep brain structure and human instinct. Like their classical forbearers, contemporary linguists acknowledge that language rules exist, but rather than focusing on how language can be corralled and limited by a few set dos and don'ts, language thinkers today are intrigued by how just a few principles allow for the nearly infinite possibilities of human language and, perhaps more importantly, how those expansive possibilities for making language are ultimately what make us human.

8. *"One Good Deed Deserves Another"*

Back when we lived in Lubbock, and I was still trying to work through my prejudice of the West Texas drawl, I volunteered as an assistant minister at my church, and I got to know a man named Joe who'd lived most of his adult life on the street. By most metrics of how one should or shouldn't live their life, Joe was having a rough go of things. He'd flunked out of school young, gotten himself kicked out of the army, and had a criminal record colorful enough to make getting steady employment next to impossible. On top of that, he rarely bathed, sported a neck tattoo, occasionally started sentences with the phrase, "I'm not racist, but . . . ," and spoke with such a thick drawl that I sometimes had trouble understanding him. If we'd crossed paths on the bus or in a dark alley in the city instead of at church, I probably would have avoided him. As it was, I spent several months working with Joe, giving him rides to doctors' appointments, taking him grocery shopping once a week, and helping him fill out a few job applications. And as happens when you spend real time getting to know someone that you might otherwise prejudge, Joe and I became friends. He told me stories about living on the street, about getting kicked out of the army, and about spending some time in jail. But he also told me about growing up in the country, about how much he liked working on cars, and the plans he had for opening his own lawn care business. I watched him take in stray animals, offer his couch to homeless friends, and even though he often resorted to panhandling for money on the street, I saw him repeatedly give away food and cash almost any time he got his hands on some.

I was in graduate school at the time, swimming in debt and worry about the future and the infinite ways I could screw it up; I knew how hard it was to think about anything with my wallet empty, so Joe's generosity perplexed me. There were clear steps he needed to take in order to get on his feet, clear rules he needed to follow. When I asked him about his generosity and we talked about his goals and the importance of careful planning and spending, he just shrugged. "Here's how I see it," he told me. "I've lived on those streets, and I know how hard it is to think about anything when your stomach is empty." What I had failed to see in all my time with Joe was that he and I were operating according to different realms of possibility when it came to goodness. Mine was wrapped up in self-preservation, self-interest, and the belief that if we learn to speak and act in a certain way, the system will eventually work. His, on the other hand, seemed based on the premise that life is too short and the system too fickle for anyone to invest too heavily in self-interest. In my mind, Joe needed to take care of Joe before he could take care of other people, but to Joe it seems, that dichotomy was a false one.

9. "It's All Good."

Turns out, the I'm-good-versus-I'm-well debate comes from a misunderstanding of verb types and is as arbitrary as any English language prescription out there. Its origins are foggy, but the logic behind the rule is clear enough. In English, adjectives modify nouns, and adverbs modify verbs. Consider the following examples:

> *I am a good person*, [*good* is an adjective; *person* is a noun. Very nice.]

but I can't

> *speak English good*. [*Speak* is a verb, so *good* has no business trying to modify it. Bad *good*.]

I can only

> *speak English well*. [*Speak* is a verb just waiting to be modified by a nice young adverb like *well*. And they live happily ever after.]

When one applies this logic to the sentence "I am good," we arrive at our usage problem. If *I* is the subject, and *am* is the verb, then *good* is no good, because *good* is an adjective, and using an adjective to modify a verb is no bueno.

However, according to Mignon Fogarty, (a.k.a. "Grammar Girl," from quickanddirtytips.com) as well as a handful of other usage mavens on the internet, *am* is a special verb. It belongs to a fraternity of sixty or so verbs called linking verbs—*feels*, *looks*, and *seems*, for instance—and unlike other verbs, which are busy describing activities, linking verbs have only one job: linking subjects, such as *The cat*, to predicates, such as *feels soft*. A few other examples:

> *This illustration* [subject] *looks wonky* [predicate].
> *This example* [subject] *seems a bit drawn-out* [predicate].

And, as it happens,

> *I* [subject] *am good* [predicate].
> (Thanks for asking.)

Incidentally, when one friend asks another, "How are you?" most contemporary grammarians worth their weight in dictionaries will say that "I am well" is the preferred answer only if the two friends in question are talking specifically about health. So, when my custodian friend flinched at his own supposedly improper use of "I am good," he was not only *good*, he was just fine, unless he was referring to his recovery from a recent hip operation or abscessed tooth, and since I know him (literally) only in passing, I think it's safe to say he wasn't giving me an update on his health. Though, if he'd asked me, I would have said he looked quite well.

Why? Prince of Kindness, remember?

I think the cure for any kind of overly cautious prescription about grammar or usage, then, is to remember that language is about communication, self-expression, persuasion, and, perhaps most pointedly, about art. And the artists who've created our finest works of literature figured out long ago what our contemporary linguists are only, in this century, finally emphasizing—that good language makes its own rules. Sure, there are foundational principles—essential grammars that make language recognizable and reproducible—but these are merely foundations to build on. The sage writers of our literary past—be it Shakespeare or Montaigne, Austen or Baldwin—are memorable precisely because they found new ways to make old language teach us something vital about our own humanity.

And as in language and literature, so in life. It's nearly impossible to do great things if we only manage to do what is expected of us. Siddhārtha, Moses, Jesus, Muhammad—each in his own way reinvented desire, redefined faith, reimagined love, and restructured devotion. And how? By finding their own paths, feeling toward a definition of goodness that felt alive and true. Ralph Waldo Emerson writes, "Let me admonish you, first of all, to go alone; to refuse the good models, even those which are sacred in the imagination of men, and dare to love God without mediator or veil." And Whitman, in the preface to *Leaves of Grass*: "Reexamine all you have been told at school or church or in any book, dismiss whatever insults your own soul; and your very flesh shall be a great poem and have the richest fluency not only in its words but in the silent lines of its lips and face and between the lashes of your eyes and in every motion and joint of your body."

Yes, I want my sons to mind the counsel they court in Sunday school, and in the poetry of holy texts, and in the words of wise adults (including, sometimes, me), but for all my anxiety about them and the example I may or may not be setting and the choices they have to make along the road to becoming men, would I really be happy if they merely did what I wanted them to? Certainly, I want them to be good, but I want them to be good because they are in love with the mysterious, contradictory, peculiar beauty of goodness, not because they're resigned to doing what they're told. And if I allow myself to see them more honestly, then really they're further along than I often give them credit for. My youngest son may be a pathological liar when it comes to whether or not he's brushed his teeth, but he loves to make cards for his friends, and he rushes out to meet me every day when I come home from work. He's quick with hugs and apologies, and he delights in bugs and pancake breakfasts and Play-Doh; and the one in the middle sometimes sulks like Eeyore and has an allergy to speaking up for himself, but he also has an uncanny instinct for the emotional needs of younger children. Whenever his little cousin comes over, he's right there on the floor with him playing games or helping him climb into a laundry basket so he can scoot him all over the house. And my oldest, while he is occasionally the perfect picture of a distant teenage boy, often surprises me with his good nature and willingness to work—dropping everything to help me run an errand or deliver something to a neighbor. Recently I caught him washing dishes late at night, and when I offered to help, he simply smiled and said, "I got this."

In such moments, part of me wants to take a bit of credit for their goodness, but that's only fair if I also take the blame for their less stellar moments. And the reality is, such transference is a fact of life, and it goes both ways. Melissa, me, our boys—we are bound to one another, as most families are, not merely by blood, but by habit, and by the inevitable education that comes with spending so much of our lives together. We are all on the same path, and they're simply figuring out for themselves what we must all figure out—that for whatever religious, moral, or ethical prescriptions we were or were not taught as children, true goodness is a type of human divinity, and we must evolve toward it.

The psychologist John Gottman is credited for identifying a "magic ratio" to govern the health of every family relationship. That is to say, the good we do to each other must outnumber the bad, and Gottman has calculated the actual ratio—five to one—and I'm told the ratio is even higher when it comes to teenagers. As I think about the good I want to do in the world, Gottman's theory gives me pause, but also offers me hope. Pause because I know how easy it has been for me, in the course of writing this, to recall the many mistakes I've made as a parent, but hope because according to Gottman, failure is a given. In the process of our becoming, we are not alone, and we do not have to be perfect. Rather, we have each other to learn from, and we need only to be good, or at least good enough.

Stuck

A million freemen may yet inhabit those counties which, while their wealth lay hidden, were disregarded for more fertile parts, but which, when developed, will furnish forth the wealth of an empire.
—CHARLES WALKER, *The History of Athens County, Ohio*, 1869

I walked through the double doors of the plasma center at eleven in the morning, right behind a man who looked like he'd just spent the night in his car. His hair leaned hard to one side of his head, and his oversized T-shirt hung low beneath the trim of his bomber jacket. I stood in line behind him at the reception desk and looked around the room. I had imagined a rusty, back-alley nightmare of cracked linoleum, flickering fluorescents, blood-stained lab coats, and crumpled dollar bills—the grime beneath the folds of Darwinian capitalism. Instead, I was greeted by starched lab coats, bleached teeth and tight ponytails, waxed floors, and a computer-automated check-in system—the highly polished face of a multibillion-dollar industry. I watched the receptionist give instructions to the man at the counter. Then she waved me forward.

I read waivers and signed forms and stood for my picture. She took my weight on a digital scale and then led me to a touch-screen computer console where I answered a long questionnaire, mostly concerning my history of sexual contact with drug users and prostitutes. I pushed the "no" button over and over, except on the questions "Are you male?" and "Are you feeling healthy and well today?"

After I completed the questionnaire, another young woman in a white coat pricked my finger and measured my iron and protein levels and then took my blood pressure and temperature before sending me to the nurse for a physical, where a woman in blue scrubs checked my balance, asked about tattoos and drug use, and lectured me briefly on getting plenty of protein and fluids. Then she led me to an empty place in a row of brown, vinyl reclining beds situated at the rear of the donation center.

None of my fellow donors, already hooked to their donation machines, looked up when I arrived. A few read from books or magazines. One held a portable DVD player in his lap. Another had his face buried in his phone, and another just lay there, one arm in her lap and the other at her side, her forearm turned upward to expose a vein. A single crimson tube draped low from her elbow toward the ground and then arced back up into a machine that clicked and beeped at her side.

"Lie down," said the young woman in the white coat, but with the sweet Appalachian lilt of her voice, I could have sworn I heard, "Make yourself at home."

Once upon a time, southeast Ohio had the largest coal deposits in the world. At its peak, the coal industry extracted more than fifty-five million tons of coal a year from more than one thousand mines around the state. For decades coal from the region fueled American industry and brought thousands of immigrants to the Appalachian countryside. They settled in small villages that grew up around the mines and breathed economic life into a region of the country long overshadowed by more promising territory to the west.

Of course, Melissa and I didn't know any of this when we moved to Athens, Ohio, a college town built on the western edge of the Appalachian range. We'd both grown up in Oregon, less than two hours from the Pacific Ocean, and we went to college in northern Utah. Droughts, endangered salmon, BLM land, and wolf repopulation schemes were a normal part of our local-news reality. East of the Mississippi might as well have been east of the Nile.

What I did know about Ohio came from memories of my high school history books and those large pull-down maps that hung above classroom chalkboards. I could picture Lake Erie and the great dipping curve of the Ohio River, and I knew that the land in between had been the nation's first notion of a western frontier, but that's about it.

As for Appalachia, I knew even less, mere caricature: Hatfields and McCoys, trailer parks and drawled speech, kids named Billy Bob, and family trees that didn't fork. For us, coming to southeast Ohio was nothing more than a means to an end, a brief stop for graduate school on the way to somewhere else. I had never once thought about the people who'd come before me, or why they might have chosen to stay.

Reclining in my donor bed, I watched Jason, the phlebotomist, move from machine to machine with a grace and offhandedness that surprised me. As he checked meters and unwrapped tubes, he rattled off the details of the donation process. Plasmapheresis, he called it, explaining that he would insert a needle into my arm, and the blood would start flowing into the large, almond-colored machine standing beside my bed. He explained that the machine would separate the plasma from my blood in a centrifuge and then pump the residual red blood cells back into my body. He warned me that I might get a metallic taste in my mouth, that I must keep pumping my hand or the machine would stop working, and, finally, that despite blinking lights and warning systems built into the machine, there was a slight chance that air might enter a vein, which could make me terribly sick or possibly even kill me. Then he placed a clipboard in my hand and said, "Just sign here that you heard me explain that."

The first white settlers came to southeast Ohio in 1787, led by a Revolutionary War veteran named Rufus Putnam. He had the ear of President Washington and the entire Northwest Territory to choose from, but instead of Lake Erie to the north, the fertile Miami River Valley to the west, or some economically strategic location closer to Pittsburgh, Rufus and his men chose the tumbling, rolling countryside of southeast Ohio. Other settlers called Putnam crazy, but he had a vision for the region that included a bustling metropolis on the banks of the Ohio River and an economy fed by rich farmland and a thriving fur trade. His advertisements described a "delightful region . . . of a much better quality than any other known to New England," and for that first exhibition he signed up sixty men. Still, Ohio proved a hard sell for most would-be immigrants. Even after treaties were forced on indigenous communities, even after forts and mills were constructed, even after plans for a university were introduced, only the most desperate and adventurous settlers were willing to take the risk.

I had not planned on donating plasma in Ohio, but the impossible math of a graduate student stipend divided by Melissa, me, and our boys inevitably added up to a visit with a financial aid officer, the small hope of a big loan, and the curious anxiety of mortgaging one's future for a chance at surviving the present. Add the specter of Christmas on the horizon, and you get a perfect formula for fatherly desperation. After just a few months in Athens, I saw a poster for the plasma center hanging on a wall at school. "Save a Life," it read, and it promised $240 a month. I was sold.

During the last decade of the eighteenth century, a slow drip of immigrants arrived in Ohio from the Northeast—families signing on a few at a time for a chance to test the region's potential. And, if that pace had held, Ohio might have remained for many years a sparsely populated forest of fur traders and subsistence farmers. However, shortly after the turn of the century, those farmers and fur trappers began taking notice of the coal. The Industrial Revolution turned that coal into black gold, and by the 1850s large mining interests were laying out a system of railroads to carry immigrants and equipment into the hills and carloads of coal back out. Labor came from England, Wales, Scotland, Czechoslovakia, Poland, and elsewhere, and by 1884 there were more than twenty thousand miners and their families scattered around the region. A man whose children might have starved in the old country could swing a pick underground in Ohio for a few dollars a week, chipping away at a vein of coal so deep and so thick it would take a legion of men two lifetimes to remove.

I have good veins, the kind inexperienced phlebotomists dream of at night. Protruding from my forearms "like garden hoses," according to one employee, they make easy targets for even the shakiest hand. Thankfully, Jason didn't need the extra help. "Don't worry," he said, as he held up the needle. "I've been doing this for years." He tapped my arm, slid the needle under my skin, and just like that I became a donor, plugged in and pumping away.

While the machine processed my plasma, I read from my book, kept my fist pumping, and occasionally looked up at the other donors around me. The man with the DVD player chuckled at something on his screen while the man with the cell phone appeared to be sending a long text message, and the woman holding nothing still stared blankly into space. Our machines hummed along, and every few minutes a finished donor and a pale orange bottle of plasma would leave, and a new donor with an empty bottle would fill the void.

After about an hour I'd donated my quota, and then the machine pumped the leftover red blood cells back into my veins for a final time, followed by a five-hundred-milliliter chaser of saline solution to boost my blood volume and keep me from fainting. On my way out, a nurse handed me a debit card loaded with twenty dollars and told me I could come back twice a week for as long as I could handle it.

Mining in Ohio was a good living, if you could handle the work. Small towns near remote mine entrances all around southeast Ohio were full of immigrants who thought they could. The towns went by simple names like Coal Run and Buckhorn; family names like Murray, Buchtel, and Mudoc; and optimistic names like New Philadelphia, New Lexington, and New Pittsburgh: places where people could start fresh, chase the dream of getting ahead, and, in reality, spend a lot of time just hanging on. Companies built shack housing and paid employees in scrip—play money that miners could use only at company stores. The hours were long and the system parasitic—the success of some mines determined less by the amount of coal extracted from the ground and more by the dollar value of the scrip that never left company property. Many mining families lived on-site, worked on-site, shopped on-site, and, if the town lasted long enough, died on-site.

Just across the street from the plasma center stood a Walmart. It wasn't the only shop in town, but sometimes it felt that way. Sure, Athens had a Kroger, a Big Lots, a Lowe's, and a few other smaller stores, but no matter how we tried to avoid it, we ended up at Walmart at least once a week. Lightbulbs, Band-Aids, diapers, milk, cereal, paint, shoelaces—they were all cheaper at Walmart. And its proximity to the plasma center made shopping there that much easier. More than a few times I left a donation session only to pull across the street to the Walmart and drop everything I'd just earned on a few groceries. And there at Walmart, more than anywhere else in town, I ran into employees from the plasma center. On the way to work or just getting off, they too made the requisite Walmart stop. Sometimes we waved or exchanged silent nods, but usually we just kept our heads down, closed off in our own little worlds.

Coal mining was not for the claustrophobic. It meant working in dark, low tunnels hundreds of feet underground for long hours with nothing but your partner, your light, and the rats to keep you company. It meant tight quarters and an ever-present fear that a fire might break out, a pillar might snap, or a shaft might seal itself off in a crumbling cloud of dust and rubble. On a Friday morning in April 1856, the pillars of a mine shaft near Blue Rock, Ohio, collapsed, trapping four miners beneath several hundred feet of dirt and rock. Fellow miners dug for days, and, near the end of the second week, they heard voices coming from beneath them. By the time the men had been pulled to safety, they'd spent more than fourteen days buried alive, trapped in an underground air pocket with nothing to drink but a bit of murky water collecting in a pool on the floor of the mine shaft. I imagine the entire town heaving a collective sigh of relief when their men emerged from the mine, but what could those men do but dust themselves off and go back to work?

Once during my predonation screening, while the attendant was checking my protein levels in a microscope, I asked her if she'd ever seen any accidents at the clinic.

"What do you mean, 'accidents'?" she said.

"You know, something goes wrong with a donor."

"Sometimes we have people pass out," she said. "A few times a year." Apparently, the majority of problems occur while a person is simply *reading* about donating. They turn white in the face, get shaky, vomit, and sometimes lose consciousness altogether. One woman became so frightened by the sight of an unwrapped needle that she gasped and ran out of the front door.

Later, while lying in my donor bed, my machine began to beep. It was a familiar sound. "Just an air bubble," said the phlebotomist. Two or three times during a donation, the plasmapheresis machine detects the presence of air somewhere in its blood line and shuts down until a phlebotomist comes and pushes a few buttons to purge the system.

"I think I can handle an air bubble," I said, but the phlebotomist gave me a funny look.

"You think you can handle air bubbles?"

"I mean . . . I can handle the beeping," I said, and she stopped at the foot of my bed.

"Well," she laughed. "The nurse does say it takes at least ten milliliters of air to kill you." She said this in a voice that was, I think, supposed to sound reassuring.

Families in mining towns lived at the mercy of the companies they worked for—the steady flow of coal their only reassurance against poverty, hunger, and cold. If an accident or strike or dried-up mine rendered a town unprofitable, the company could pack up and go, leaving the men and their families to find other ways of making do.

In 1920 a coal processing structure burned to the ground in San Toy, a small mining town northeast of Athens. More than 2,500 people had moved to San Toy since its founding in 1901. The company town boasted a theater, a baseball team, and a hospital, but instead of rebuilding after the fire, the Sunday Creek Mine Company shut down one mine and eventually withdrew from the city completely. Within eight years the town was empty. What equipment could be salvaged was distributed to other nearby mines, and the hundreds of displaced workers had little choice but to pick up and follow the equipment, leaving behind a ghost town, a tiny scar on the hillside stitched together by vacant rail lines fading slowly into the undergrowth.

After I'd donated plasma a few times, I showed my scars to Melissa: a red dot on the inside of each elbow.

"Yuck," she said and turned away, unwilling to look. I got the same response from pretty much everyone I talked to about donating. Sure, needles and blood make people squeamish, but a unique stigma lies in the act of donating itself—a choice that lies on the socioeconomic spectrum of desperation somewhere between skipping a utility payment and stealing money from a roommate. People understood why I did it, but most couldn't imagine doing it themselves.

Melissa never liked to hear me talk about donating, and she often apologized, as if the whole thing were her fault. She worried about my health, worried that months of donating would cause irrevocable damage to my body, that for the rest of my life I'd wear a solitary track mark on each forearm, my small badge of courage, a pair of misplaced stigmata—a sign to be sure, but of what?

I carried in my mind a dim awareness that a mixture of needles, blood, and money meant dirty business, but it took a bit of research to find out the details. For instance, in 1970 *Time* magazine reported that more than one hundred thousand people donated plasma regularly in the United States, most of them "Skid Row bums and drug addicts"—impoverished, desperate men and women who infected the plasma pool first with Hepatitis C and later, in the early 1980s, with HIV. For decades, the unregulated industry allowed cash-strapped drug users to donate several times a week at multiple locations without any screening or testing of collected fluids. The industry then turned that plasma into anti-coagulant medicine for hemophiliacs and blood volume boosters for trauma victims. According to some estimates, nearly twenty thousand hemophiliacs contracted HIV from tainted plasma, not to mention the thousands infected by Hepatitis C. The federal government eventually stepped in and set up proper regulations, but by then the plasma industry had secured its reputation as blood pushers and donors as the industry's blood whores.

Coal miners were rough, dirty, wild, and ignorant. Or so the mythology says. Going into the mines branded a person and gave permission to those on the surface to simultaneously pity and revile them. Underground five or six days a week, in a saloon or at a card table at night, coated in and coughing up black dust, early miners did not live genteel lives. It's easy to see how the stereotypes got their start. History books from the region overflow with photographs of miners, almost always sitting atop a mining cart, or posing by a piece of equipment, or squatting on their aluminum lunch pails, their faces stained, coal dust darkening the crow's-feet around their eyes and deepening the wrinkles in their foreheads. Theirs was a life of overalls and boots, of headlamps and thick denim, of grime and whistles and black phlegm. Almost universally, they look tired in the high-contrast of old mono-chrome photographs; and the way they lean elbows on knees, or lift hands to their hips, one gets the impression that these men were busy, that in the backs of their minds they knew that the day wouldn't be over until their carts were full. I imagine that a miner, stuck with a company tab to pay off and a family to feed, had little time for worrying about public image.

Stick is the verb of choice among phlebotomists, as in "I stuck fifteen people today" and "You can choose who sticks you" and "Who stuck you? They did it all wrong." The word choice always seemed so unfortunate to me—the one with the needle sticking out of my arm, the one stuck in the bed for an hour, the one feeling like a stuck cow attached to a milk pump.

But I don't think they meant any harm by it. I often told my phlebotomist I could never stick a needle into someone else's arm. And maybe that's why they talked about donors like we were pincushions—to dehumanize us, if just a little, to steel themselves against the reality of what they were extracting all day, and from whom.

By the late twentieth century more than 3.4 billion tons of coal had been extracted from Ohio soil. At its height the coal industry employed fifty thousand people in the state, but by the early 1990s advances in technology had so altered coal mining that fewer than five thousand employees were needed to keep the entire industry running. Today mines are safer, cleaner, and more efficient, but they are also emptier. The miner is no longer the most efficient tool in the mine, which means Appalachian boys whose fathers grew up to be miners because their fathers had grown up to be miners have had to come up with new plans for the future.

Since the early 1990s, the plasma industry has worked hard to transform the donating process into the reassuringly sterile experience I endured in Ohio. Back when I was donating, three hundred plasma centers in the United States collected around fifteen million liters a year. In a decade the number of plasma centers has doubled, and the amount of collected plasma has almost tripled. Sure, the process is, for the most part, streamlined, safe, and secure. In fact, donating feels as routine as a trip through Jiffy Lube, with someone guiding you through every step of the process, minding the fluids and hoses while you sit and read a magazine. But for as reliable as the industry has become, plasma companies still target poor neighborhoods and run their business on the very old notion that it's okay to expect the underemployed and under-privileged to sacrifice their bodies on the altar of economic survival.

Some evenings in Athens I sat beside a woman who made her donations on the way to a night shift at Taco Bell; other evenings it was a man just getting off work at Walmart. I met hard-up college students and single parents and migrant workers. I talked with folks who used the money to supplement their food stamps or unemployment checks, and on Saturdays I donated with parents who dropped off their kids at the "supervised waiting room" to watch a Disney movie while Mom and Dad earned that extra bit of cash. Of course, I didn't really know much about any of these donors or their particular financial situations, but we were donating plasma in one of the poorest counties in the country, a place where even a little money can mean a great deal, so it isn't difficult to imagine the value they might have placed on an extra sixty dollars a week.

I knew what it meant for me—a little cushion, a temporary buffer between today and the end of the month, an excuse to get dessert at Applebee's, to put an extra gift under the tree, or pay for gas to Cleveland. We needed the money, to be sure, but the poverty we felt was somewhat artificial. We had a little money in the bank, more student loan options than we knew what to do with, and I was working on a graduate degree. Donating was never an act of true desperation. I came here to Ohio for school, and school would be my ticket out.

And perhaps this idea of *getting out* is what first had me thinking about the parallels between plasma donation and coal mining, about poverty and the need for escape, about finding oneself at the mercy of big business and doing whatever it takes to survive. Times have been decidedly tough for a lot of people in southeast Ohio for a very long time, and economic solutions are neither simple nor sure. The longer my family lived there, the more we got to know the little towns and villages that persisted in the region, the more boarded up schools we passed, the more news stories we read about drug use and high school dropout rates, the more questions I had about why anyone would stay in place with such dismal prospects for education, work, and stability. And I might chalk up such an oversimplification of the entire region's economic outlook to my age and inexperience, but I know it reflected a larger, more problematic class-based delusion about the relative ease of social mobility and some fundamental cluelessness about the challenges of systemic poverty, not to mention the myriad other reasons apart from money that people choose to stay settled in a place. At the time though, I couldn't help but focus on the dark notion that hard times might reach out and grab me, that I was just one injury, illness, or failed job interview from donating plasma for the rest of my life, and in the face of that possibility I knew only one thing—I had no intention of getting stuck.

In the spring, Melissa and I took our boys to see the old train depot in Murray City, a defunct mining town tucked back into the hills north of Athens. The drive took about twenty minutes on narrow, winding roads that cut through green-leaf forests, pocked by the occasional trailer or farm home. Murray City itself emerged from the woods first as a series of small houses, and then a new fire station beside a park, and finally as a few larger brick buildings, including a boarded-up high school, a convenience store, a bar, and an Elks Lodge. Beyond that were clusters of small houses and, at the end of town, an old train depot recently converted into a small mining museum. Beside the depot sat a large red caboose that helped complete the picture of a little train stop in the middle of the woods. We parked in a gravel lot next to the depot and climbed out of the car. Across the parking lot was a long narrow greenway that I could tell had once been the train line.

The mines around Murray City were at one time among the highest-yielding coal mines in the world, and that success meant great things for the growing town and its more than two thousand citizens. There were schools, churches, banks, retail stores, a newspaper called the *Murray City News*, a labor union, and four trains a day that steamed through the small depot. One dollar and twenty-five cents could get you to Columbus for the weekend, but why would you want to leave? Wake up on a Saturday morning and you could visit the doctor, take your kids to the park, and pick up some produce at Lunt's Groceries, all before noon. Then you could get your hair cut at the barbershop on Locust Street and still have time to see a show at the theater or watch the Murray City Tigers wallop a neighboring town on the gridiron. At night you could buy a friend a drink at one of twenty-three saloons, and on Sunday morning you could catch a sermon from one of five different pulpits. The coal brought the people, and the people built the town, and the town became the center of life for hundreds of miners and their families for nearly half a century.

Looking through the museum's old photographs of parades and marching bands and city councilmen in sharp bowler hats, it was easy to imagine a happy life in Murray. And it was easy to see why some residents would resort to violence to defend that life. The first labor strikes occurred at the Murray mines in 1884. Locals wanted better pay, and companies wanted more output, and that tension roiled up every few years for decades. Striking miners set fires, destroyed company property, and even fired shots at foreign scabs brought in to work the mines. But, amid all this, Murray managed to survive. Even after World War II, when strip mining was rapidly replacing underground operations and Murray's mines began to close, the city didn't fold. Not completely. Even when the last picks and shovels were hauled away, more than a few people stayed put, deciding to commute to whatever job came next rather than sell their land and look for something new.

Today, about 450 people live in Murray City. There is no bank, no newspaper, and no grocery store—and all but one of the churches has been shuttered. All the children in town are bused to schools in other cities, and those adults who are not elderly or retired must commute to Nelsonville, Athens, or farther, for work. Other than the depot and the grassed-over railbed, the only hint of the city's mining past was inscribed on a plaque in a park built over an old mine entrance.

My boys poked around the museum for a few minutes, asking questions about old photographs and train tickets and a large bucket of coal in the corner, but they grew restless. We went outside and let them climb on the red caboose, snapping photos as they posed against the overcast sky. When we pulled up to the museum that morning, I wondered aloud to Melissa why anyone would live way out in such impossible quiet. But the quiet my boys sat in as I took their photo was not the quiet of a ghost town. The forests around us laid benevolent siege to the little village in the way only an Appalachian forest can, and I felt both secluded and nestled in a strange way. In that moment, the silent, wet world of the woods was enough of a reason for Murray to persist. Before we left we climbed inside the caboose and sat on the cracked seats and looked out the window at the tracks below—tracks that had been restored just for this little memorial: two beams of oxidized steel coming in from nowhere to hold up the bright old caboose and then quitting just beyond the car's front coupler, a heavy, steel hook that seemed to punctuate the town's only question: "Going so soon?"

One day at the plasma center, a young couple walked through the door as I tapped out my questionnaire on the computer. The man wore a pair of vintage Air Jordans and jean shorts with the words *mi raza* embroidered down one leg. Tattoos wrapped around both his forearms and around both calves, and he spoke loudly on his cell phone in a thick West Virginia drawl. The woman had blond, curly hair, and a strip of her midriff peeked out beneath the hem of her white tank top. They couldn't have been older than twenty. I watched as the woman stood on the scale and then heard the attendant give her the bad news.

"Hundred and eight," she said. "You have to weigh at least one-ten."

The man rolled his eyes, and I heard him explain the situation to the person on the phone—he had been cleared for donation, but the woman would have to wait out front.

A few minutes later I was all plugged in, and the man on the phone sat a few beds over, still talking loudly.

"A house and a double-wide," I heard him say. "We only pay utilities." He paused for a moment and then raised his voice: "That's what I'm talking about," he said. "Appalachian Ohio is the poorest place in the United States, man." He raised his voice again and continued, "'Cause there ain't no jobs!" And he went on for several minutes about his struggle to find work, his hopes for starting a business, his affinity for good pot, and his frustration with the cops who wouldn't leave him alone. "It's like no one's free up here!" he yelled. But then his voice softened, and he said,

"But it's beautiful, dude. Come up here in the summertime. It's beautiful."

And it was these sorts of encounters that made me reconsider my wariness of Ohio: meeting men for whom Appalachia was home in the deepest, most sentimental way possible, men whose families had lived in the region for generations—who knew what it took to put down roots and what it meant to pull them up. I had spent the better part of a year coming to the condescending conclusion that men like this were simply victims of circumstance, products of their region's own troubled history, stuck as much by geography as genealogy. And sure, you might call what I heard in his voice anxiety, maybe even a little desperation, but when he said, "Come up here in the summertime. It's beautiful," his voice hinted at something else—less fear of what a place might take from him and more faith in what it might have to offer. It was a voice that trusted in the hidden promises of a sleepy Appalachian hollow, a voice he might have heard first from his father, or his father's father, a voice that sounded that day like an invitation. And perhaps it was something like that voice that called us to Ohio in the first place, that got me into that donor bed and selling myself a few hundred milliliters of plasma at a time, a voice that asks us to suspend judgment, to take courage, to bet on the path beneath our feet; a voice from beyond history that calls men and women to settle strange lands and offer their own pound of flesh for a chance at life; a voice that says, "Come and stay awhile—see what happens," a voice that has echoed in these hills for a very long time.

White Trash

Let me take you back to one of the more visceral memories of my childhood. I'm fourteen or maybe fifteen years old, and it's pretty late on a cold autumn evening in Portland, Oregon—the kind of cold that makes you want to drive with the windows up and the heater on high. But that won't do because Mom and I are tearing along Farmington Road in her red Nissan Sentra, the backseat is piled high with bags of trash, and if I roll up the windows the smell might overwhelm us. "Wear a jacket," she'd told me, but I didn't listen, and the whole drive I shiver in the breeze.

She called these trips "garbage runs," and though they felt clandestine enough to me, she'd balk at the notion we were doing anything illegal. Yes, we were hauling a car full of household trash to a dumpster at her office, and no, we didn't have permission from anyone to do so, but she'd worked at that office for years, and she knew the building manager paid a flat fee for those dumpsters, whether they were full or not. To her, that was the important detail—the one that led her at some point during my middle school years to stop paying the city garbage fee and instead let the trash bags pile up in our garage each week until Thursday night rolled around; then she'd announce that we were going on a garbage run. She'd pull her Sentra up to our garage door, swing open the hatch, lay out a blue tarp over the folded seats, and then we'd gingerly stack the plastic bags in the back of the wagon, careful to keep them tied and intact—this was the family car after all. Summer or winter we drove with the windows down, and though the drive lasted only a few minutes, the smell seemed to linger for days.

My dad fancies himself a genealogy buff, and he never tires of reminding the family that we had ancestors on the *Mayflower*— not just one, but several. He puts a lot of stock in our Pilgrim blood and the familiar founding myth of Europeans in North America—Puritan, Quaker, and Lutheran free men risking it all for religious liberty in an untamed wilderness across the sea. These are our people, or so the story goes. The truth, of course, is more telling, if not nearly as romantic. Sure a few lines of our genealogy may trace themselves back to the deck of the *Mayflower*, and to the powerbrokers and landholders of the young Plymouth plantation, but in my family tree, for every "who's-who-in-American-history," there are shiploads of anonymous laborers whose primary reasons for emigrating from Europe had at least as much to do with poverty as any sort of piety.

Consider the economic reality for sixteenth- and seventeenth-century working-class folks in England and really anywhere in Europe. Populations were booming, employment was scarce, land was even scarcer, and religious and political revolution bubbled beneath the surface. Between 1500 and 1700 London's population grew from fifty thousand to five hundred thousand. Prisons and workhouses were overflowing, and the streets were crawling with the orphaned, the vagrant, and the hungry. These poor were seen as "idle," "disease-ridden" vagabonds who placed an undue burden on the rest of society. In *White Trash: The 400-Year Untold History of Class in America*, historian Nancy Isenberg describes how the poor were seen as human waste: "Waste people, like waste lands, were stagnant; their energy produced nothing of value," and as is often the case with society's trash, few cared what happened to it, as long as it was out of sight—and mind.

Talking with my mother now, it appears she has blocked out most memories of our weekly garbage runs. She certainly doesn't remember when the idea popped into her mind, and when I pressed her, she admitted that maybe she'd led the occasional trip to the dumpsters—but only with grass clippings or a load of oversized items. I insisted that these trips were normal, that she'd come home one day and announced the scheme to all of us over dinner. I reminded her of how we piled up the trash bags in the garage and of our late-night drives with the windows down. "We made the trip every week for years," I told her. "You don't remember?" Mom listened to my story, and then she shrugged. "Yeah, that sounds about right," she said. "We were broke pretty much all the time back then, and every little bit helped."

According to Nancy Isenberg, the aristocracy of Elizabethan England believed that the poor were a drag on society and that nature would deal with them in one way or another: the weakest among them would die of illness or starvation. Others would be conscripted into war and die on the battlefield or at sea, and still others would fall into the criminal class and die in prison or by the hangman's noose. The New World, writes Isenberg, would provide a fourth way. Instead of dying in the streets or hanging from the gallows, these "wastrels" of British society could hitch a ride on a merchant ship and sail to a land of opportunity. In fact, England's poor were part of the colonization plan from the beginning. Isenberg tells of a well-connected London lawyer named Richard Hakluyt who, in 1584, wrote "A Discourse Concerning Western Planting," in which he outlined his theory for how "petty thieves" and the children of "wandering beggars," who would otherwise "grow up idly and hurtful and burdenous" to England, could instead be "condemned for certain years in the western parts," to either pay their debt to society or secure a chance at freedom. Colonial bosses would take Hakluyt's idea and mechanize it. Over the next century and a half, hundreds of thousands of Britons and other Europeans were sold into servitude to provide cheap labor for the plantations and pastures of the American colonies. These were "free-willers" who volunteered themselves into servitude in order to pay their way across the ocean, but these were also the "surplus people" of Europe, write Don Jordan and Michael Walsh. These were children sent by desperate parents or "spirited" into servitude by company agents and greedy ship captains. These were thieves, drunks, brawlers, and prostitutes who were offered labor in the colonies to avoid jail or execution. These were political enemies in Ireland and former soldiers with no work. In a 1622 sermon John Donne lays out the benefit of the colonial immigration program: "It shall sweep your streets, and wash your doors from idle persons, and the children of idle persons, and employ them," he writes. The colonies would be the kingdom's "spleen, to drain the ill humors of the body" but also "a liver, to breed good blood." As Isenberg explains, colonized America was "a place where surplus poor, the waste people of England, could be converted into economic assets. The land and the poor could be harvested together, to add to—rather than continue to subtract from—the nation's wealth."

If Mom hated anything, it was waste—wasted energy, wasted time, and wasted money. Which makes sense because my father worked only sporadically for much of their marriage, and supporting the family largely fell to her. Having her first child at sixteen and her seventh child at forty meant Mom spent the better part of six decades waging a pitched battle against poverty, perpetually experimenting with new ways to stretch a dollar and use her time more efficiently. She bought food staples in five-gallon buckets to get the bulk discount. She cut fresh milk with powdered to make it go farther. She trolled neighborhoods looking for unkempt fruit trees and knocked on doors to get permission to pick the cherries or apples or pears before they went bad. I once spent half a Saturday fifteen feet up a cherry tree growing in the middle of a dentist's office parking lot picking large clumps of fruit and tossing them down to Mom who alternated between warnings ("Be careful up there") and encouragement ("Can you reach a little higher?"). She canned the fruit, boiled it into jam, pressed it for juice, and dried it into fruit leather on screens that she set out on the roof. On Saturdays she baked sausage rolls by the dozens and froze them in gallon-sized bags for all the kids to snack on during the week. She became a maven of macaroni casseroles, mixing the elbow pasta with everything from tomato sauce and ground beef to mayonnaise and canned tuna. At Thanksgiving when turkeys went on sale, she bought as many as would fit in the freezer, and after cooking and carving a bird, she'd boil down the carcass to make soup broth and freeze it for later.

She shopped at thrift stores for clothes and used her sewing machine to make us Halloween costumes, pajamas, quilts, and even formal wear. My oldest sister remembers the sewing machine humming all afternoon the day of a big dance and Mom putting in the final stitches just before my sister's date showed up. She bought us bicycles from obscure discount shops on the far side of town, inherited furniture from neighborhood move-outs, purchased automobiles from repo auctions, collected newspapers and soda cans to recycle for money at the local reclamation plant, and took odd jobs to fill in the gaps where her dollar wouldn't stretch: she drove a paper route, ran a small business selling pizzas to the neighborhood, operated an ad hoc day care, and even started a booth at the local farmer's market where she put us kids to work selling fried bread and cotton candy. And even though she never graduated from high school, she worked her way up from a filing job at a local law firm, eventually becoming a certified right-of-way agent who reviews multimillion-dollar projects going on all over the country.

If anyone today ever tries to point out the extent of her suburban street hustle, however, Mom says, simply, "I did what I had to do."

"Survival" is the word that comes to mind most readily when I imagine the preoccupations of those early colonial servants in my family tree. For the privilege of a two-month ship passage on perilous Atlantic seas, most indentured servants were contracted for several years to a master whom they agreed to serve "well and faithfully [in] such employments as the master might assign." The lucky served under benevolent masters for three to nine years and then were sent on their way with some bushels of corn, a bit of money, and maybe some acreage. The unlucky were overworked and underfed, beaten, raped, sold to other landholders, and sometimes killed. The most desperate escaped to some other colony or out into the wilderness. All were essentially economic pawns in a grand money-making scheme that enriched investors and speculators back in England and created wealthy dynasties out of the relatively small group of new-world landholders who ruled from the North Atlantic coast to the Caribbean.

Historian Abbot Emerson Smith figures that only two in ten indentured servants went on to husband their own land or profit from some sort of trade or paid labor. These were the "sound and solid" few, writes Smith, the success stories who worked the land or developed a trade and would contribute not only to the prosperous future of their individual families but would, in their own small ways, help forge the founding myth of an America built by free, industrious Englishmen with the wind of liberty at their backs and the providence of God on their side. The other 80 percent, writes Smith, "either died during their servitude, returned to England after it was over," or became part of what historian Kenneth Morgan describes as "the underbelly of poor white workers in the colonies." "They were not sturdy pioneers," writes Smith. "They were shiftless, hopeless, ruined individuals" who could scarcely hope to provide for themselves, let alone their posterity.

When it came to providing for her family, Mom's ingenuity often impressed me, but it also made me self-conscious. I didn't like being the kid with the hand-me-down jacket who stood sheepishly in line at school every Monday to pick up the red "free lunch" tickets, while it seemed the kids all around me were picking up the normal green ones. When she made sausage rolls I wished for Hot Pockets, and I could barely bring myself to eat her macaroni casseroles. I grimaced at the noises that came from all those auction-repo vehicles—the scream of timing belts, the sputter of congested carburetors, and the grinding of metal-worn brakes. I hated the generic labels of the church-relief food in our pantries, the sat-on look of all our used furniture, and, of course, those garbage runs—how nervous and conspicuous I felt slinging trash bags from the back of our wagon into that dumpster while the headlights of her Sentra blazed in the darkness. I hated how much I worried that some neighbor might call the police or that trash might spill out into the car and make the rotten-milk smell permanent. Looking back, I don't know where this sense of entitlement came from on my part, but I know it had to do with my wealthy friends and their seemingly ideal nuclear families—families with new cars that emitted no undesirable noises or smells, their bright pantries overflowing with store-bought goodies. All those stay-at-home moms perpetually baking chocolate chip cookies and an army of fathers with salaried nine-to-five jobs, well-groomed lawns, vegetable gardens, and two-week vacations to Hawaii.

I had poor friends, too, who lived more hand-to-mouth than we ever did, but it was the wealthy ones that got into my head. What would it be like, I often wondered, to have been born into one of those families?

In his 1931 book, *The Epic of America*, James Truslow Adams described the United States as "a land in which life should be better and richer and fuller for everyone, with opportunity for each according to ability or achievement." He called this vision the American Dream and wrote the following: "It is not a dream of motor cars and high wages merely, but a dream of social order in which each man and each woman shall be able to attain to the fullest stature of which they are innately capable, and be recognized by others for what they are, regardless of the fortuitous circumstances of birth or position." In short, the American Dream is one of upward mobility—but not *only* upward mobility. Here Adams, like so many American idealists before him and since, attempts to excise America from any sort of class system, and set it into an imaginary egalitarian meritocracy where everyone, through their "innate capability," has a chance to succeed. Of course, the very notion of upward mobility presupposes a class system—a social ladder that needs climbing. This may be the most fundamental dilemma in America—the social ladder doesn't simply touch ground anywhere you want it to. Instead, you have to know where to find it, and you need someone to help you make the climb. Innate capability gets you only so far. Success takes support—family, friends, pastors, good schools, watchful neighbors, freedom to move and do as you like. This dilemma reveals a troubling contradiction—the American Dream promises that you and I can, through hard work and determination, improve our social standing; but then it simultaneously reassures us that our social standing doesn't matter in the first place. The truth, of course, is that all of us are, to a greater or lesser extent, at the mercy of where we came from, who our parents were, and what society thinks those facts say about our potential.

One way to measure the economic value of labor in seventeenth- and eighteenth-century colonial America is to consider the individual worker's potential for exploitation. The more vulnerable the labor force, the more profitable. I can picture a former convict or street orphan from London stepping down from a landing boat into the cold surf and perhaps realizing for the first time the desperate reality of the situation. Stuck between a vast wilderness and an endless ocean, people had literally nowhere else to go. What could they do but submit to their masters? And if that description sounds familiar, it should. Many scholars see the indenture system as a prototype for the African slave system that would ultimately replace it, an exploitation proving ground that taught landholders exactly what it took to control the day-to-day fate of another human being. The vast difference between the two systems? In a word: hope. Even the roughest, most poorly used English-born servant could, at least theoretically, hold out for independence at some point in the distant future. The colonial promise of land, wages, and freedom—though admittedly far off and unlikely—was possible for a white servant. For those first few thousand Africans that were enslaved in the Americas during the mid-1600s, and for the millions that would ultimately follow, life in America would be a life in chains, marked by a level of fear and uncertainty many orders of magnitude greater than anything felt by immigrants from Europe.

My mother was a sixteen-year-old girl when she married for the first time, pregnant and uncertain of her future with a boy named Ray who'd chosen to "do the right thing." When I called her to ask about the details of this difficult time in her life, she said, "I'll tell you all about it as long as I can wash dishes while we talk." So, I asked questions, and she scrubbed dishes and tried to remember.

It was 1962 when she and Ray got married, and they had no skills, no education, and no prospects. What they did have was family. Ray's dad put them up in their first apartment, and later Mom's dad helped Ray get a sheet metal apprenticeship in Las Vegas. Down in Vegas family friends helped them find cheap places to live, and when Ray decided he wanted to go into the dog-breeding business, Mom's parents loaned them the money to buy a Schutzhund-trained shepherd from Germany. By 1972 they were in business with another couple and running a successful dog kennel in downtown Las Vegas. Ray and Mom would eventually divorce, but together, and most importantly with the help of friends and family, they escaped a slip into deep poverty and made the transition from teenage parents to working adults.

What my mother described to me over the phone is a short chapter in a much longer history of support that stretches back in her family all the way to colonial times. My father may enjoy talking up the historical significance of his early-American pedigree, but my mother is the one with the stories and documentation. Mom is a Hess of Swiss and German extraction, and her ancestors came to Pennsylvania in the early 1700s as part of what was called the redemptioner system. Where English colonists often emigrated alone, German redemptioners typically traveled as families and church groups. Many sold their old-world assets to help pay for their passage to the New World, and as a result, they often started their colonial lives with more money, more family support, and less need to bind themselves in servitude than other emigrants. By the mid-1730s, those early Hess families owned substantial tracts of farmland all over southern Pennsylvania. They had wagonloads of children and spread out over the countryside, relying on the skills they'd learned from their parents, reestablishing farms, mills, pastures, and herds everywhere they went. Drive through parts of rural Pennsylvania today and you're likely to come across an old Hess homestead or one of several Hess family graveyards.

My fourth-great-grandfather left Pennsylvania in the early 1800s for cheap land in Ohio, then traveled west to Iowa, where his son went on with Latter-day Saint pioneers to the expanses of the Intermountain West. In Idaho and Utah my branch of the Hess line became dairymen, ranchers, and sheep herders. They became teachers and state legislators and religious leaders. They married and had large, close-knit families that shared orchards and pastureland. When my grandfather first married, he lived in an apartment that belonged to his father-in-law. He got work from family and church friends, and when he bought two acres in north Pocatello on installments, his father and father-in-law helped him build a house and start a garden.

Mom worked on that house and in those fields, but she also learned to cut hair and can fruit; she learned to sew and tie quilts and cook and play the piano. She learned to paint and repair the house, and she learned to love the stories and vocabulary lists in the *Reader's Digest*; she learned how to bake for the neighbors and care for grandparents and how to lean on God for support. She learned to work first and rest later, to fix things up and wear them out. Some of the Hesses managed to accumulate modest fortunes, but most were working-class folks whose wealth lay not in their bank accounts but in their solid family structures. The Hesses have, for the most part, been flush with what social scientists call cultural and social capital: skills and knowledge for success at home and work, and well-established social networks. I don't think it's a stretch to suggest that what saved my mom when she was a pregnant teenager was exactly what helped my early Hess relatives survive on the frontier of Pennsylvania.

For the system of indentured servitude to remain profitable, those who ran it needed huge plantations and a steady flow of cheap labor. Land came easy enough from driving out the indigenous population (the first stage of a slow genocide that would last three centuries), and a steady flow of sailing ships increased the European workforce by the thousands. However, as one generation of indentured servants gave way to the first generation of freeborn Americans, the colonial economy began to change. By the 1670s several colonies had been established between Maine and South Carolina, giving immigrants more choices about where they worked. At the same time, new legislation guaranteed adequate room and board for servants, prohibited overwork and abuse, and limited the length of indenture. In addition, settlement villages expanded into towns and cities with economies hungry not only for farm labor but for artisans, craftsmen, tradesmen, and overseers. With a more robust economy came longer life expectancy and an increase in marriages, children, and freemen taking up land or learning a trade.

All this progress meant one thing: the white population was becoming harder to exploit for economic gain. But what, you might ask, is a desperate landholder to do with all that acreage to work and so few white laborers willing to work it? Raise wages? Shorten indentures? Improve working conditions in some other way? All that happened to some extent, but it quickly became clear that the only way to maximize profits on these plantations would be to find another vulnerable group to exploit—and that group was already on the ground.

African labor was first brought to North America in 1619, but over the next thirty years, Africans would make up only ten thousand of the estimated eighty-five thousand members of the servant class. And though an African was bought as "a slave forever," at first some served, like their white counterparts, as indentured servants who worked for their freedom. Some married, purchased land, and even owned slaves of their own, but eventually, as the economic and political climate improved for white labor, the powers-at-be moved to solidify the African population into a lower caste. Take Virginia, for instance. Between 1660 and 1680 the commonwealth legislature passed numerous slave laws that attempted to strip the humanity from all servants of color. First they bound Black children to the labor status of their mothers—if Mom was a slave for life, so too was her child. Next they clarified that all Black people, even baptized ones, were subject to bondage. They passed corporal punishment laws that allowed masters to beat their slaves into submission, then passed laws granting immunity to any master who accidentally beat a slave to death. They outlawed slaves from carrying weapons, made it illegal for slaves to leave their plantations without permission, and declared slave resistance a capital offense. Similar laws would spring up all over the colonies, creating a web of legislation that effectively erased the humanity of Africans in the eyes of the law. As one historian put it, in Virginia, and really all over colonial North America, people of African descent "ceased to be men in whom masters held a proprietary interest and became chattels, objects that were the property of their owners."

Meanwhile, global market forces were making slave labor in North America more desirable too. In the Caribbean sugar prices were dropping, which meant plantations had less money and incentive to buy additional slaves; this created a surplus of slave labor that traders then offloaded on the mainland at cut-rate prices.

Then the Royal African Company lost its English monopoly on the slave trade, and independent traders drove the price of slaves down even further. If you were a landholder in North America looking for cheap, unskilled labor, slaves were becoming more and more appealing. And since Christian apologists had long been relying on passages from the Bible to justify slavery, it was easy enough for many to set aside any moral objections to human bondage and instead focus on the basic economic question: Why put money into white servants who would work for only a few years and then set off on their own when you could buy slaves on the cheap, work them for life, and take ownership of any children they produced? Put simply, white servants moved off the plantations to take advantage of broader economic opportunities in other parts of America, but that move was largely made possible because Black slaves were forced to take their places. This is one meaning behind the famous remark by Ta-Nehisi Coates that slaves "were this country's first windfall, the down payment on its freedom." Another way to process this uncomfortable truth— the profit-at-any-cost colonial economy required an expendable workforce, a waste class that could be used to feed the economic furnace of the New World, and if you are a white American like me, whose ancestors got their first real shot at economic freedom in the Americas, odds are, the only reason they had any sort of chance was because Black slaves had none.

I'm a tenured professor at a private university now, and looking back on the relative poverty of my childhood, I like to think I'm grateful for the sacrifices that Mom made for the family. I like to think that back then I was grateful too, that I understood what Mom was doing for all of us. But then there's this memory—some afternoon as a teenager I was working in our kitchen, perhaps making lunch or an afternoon snack, and Mom was unloading the dishwasher when she paused over the silverware drawer for a moment, considered its contents, and then picked up the tray and turned it upside down, dumping all the silverware loose into the drawer. Then she took the silverware basket from the dishwasher and dumped it into the drawer as well. She looked at me watching her and said, "This is how we're doing it now. No more tray," and she went back to her work.

I didn't think much of her move in that moment—it merely registered as another way Mom was trying to make her busy life a little easier. The scene must have stuck with me though, because a few months later I was again working in the kitchen, and maybe we'd just taken a garbage run the night before, or maybe I'd heard my parents arguing about money that week, or perhaps I'd been feeling a bit self-conscious about Dad being out of work or Mom wearing those worn-out jeans, or maybe I'd been that morning to a friend's house that always seemed so well appointed—new furniture and plush carpet, gleaming fixtures, expensive family portraits on the wall, and even an electronic trash compactor—whatever the reason, I must have been smarting under the perceived weight of my own class status because I opened that drawer in the kitchen, and I said, "Ugh, Mom, this drawer . . . ," and I struggled for a phrase to capture how I was feeling. "It's so . . . it's so *white trash*."

My mother is a kind woman—conciliatory and self-effacing. She has always taken the small slice of cake; has always been quick to apologize, quick to give the benefit of the doubt; has always been diplomatic and practical in her expressions of stress and fear, but in this moment I watched in her eyes as some switch flipped, ever so briefly, and in that nanosecond I glimpsed in my mother a rare combination of rage, sadness, embarrassment, and ultimately resolution. "Listen," she said, in a voice that meant "I love you, so I'm going to spell this out for you very slowly" but also meant "I'm about to drop some serious facts about adulthood, you ungrateful turd," and then she explained what I already knew— she was overworked at home and at the office. She couldn't make any more money than she was already making, and time was the only resource she had left to budget. "Any questions?" She asked, and of course I had none, so I pulled out the fork I was looking for and shut the drawer.

The other day I called Mom to talk about this memory, to apologize, and to ask what was really running through her head at that moment. I wanted to know if she'd felt as self-conscious about class as I did back then, but she has no memory of the exchange and no recollection of how she felt about my implication that we were "white trash." As she remembers things, she didn't have time to think about class status. "I think when you're in the middle of the struggle, you don't think on a day-to-day basis," she told me. "Everything is minute-to-minute." For Mom, as for many working poor, preoccupations with class may have been just another luxury she couldn't afford. Except that I know Mom thought about class, at least in as much as she hoped for a better future for her children. She worked as much as she did so we could have clothes for school and fees for sports and drama and Scout camps and food on the table and a house to live in. She read us poetry, sat us down in front of good movies, forced us to try new food; she taught us to clean the house, get our homework done, and shovel the neighbor's walk, and even with that silverware drawer she was teaching us what matters (time) over what doesn't (appearances). At the end of that phone conversation, she volunteered a bit of wisdom about raising children: "You want to know how I define 'high class'?" she asked. "The only mark of a high-class individual is her willingness to work hard enough to give her children more opportunities than she had."

So, what is the legacy of indentured servitude and the brutal system of slavery that followed it? In white America we often talk about indentured servants as a foundational ingredient in the bubbling soup of the American melting pot—proud, liberty-loving workers from all over Europe who came here and took the decidedly difficult, but ultimately necessary first steps in the development of our novel nation of free men. Too often, slavery gets a similar gloss—treated as just another unfortunate, but inevitable, fact of history. A relic of the Old World that our Founding Fathers begrudgingly kept alive for the good of the union, a cancer that would take a war to excise; but hey, at least we got rid of it, and all those years ago at that. Maybe the first two and a half centuries weren't so good for Black folks, but look how far they've come.

Of course, the true legacy of indentured servitude is a paradox. On the one hand, it helped plant in our social consciousness a belief in pure meritocracy—that if someone puts in the work, they'll get ahead and leave things better for their kids. But on the other hand, with that first boatload of "waste people" from England, the indenture system took for granted that some individuals would never merit anything more than a short, rough life of hard labor and deprivation. And to make such class determinism palatable, society has long branded the poorest of the poor as dirty, ignorant, and incapable of bettering themselves. They deserve what they get.

As Nancy Isenberg explains, that notion of an undeserving bottom rung of society has never left us. In *White Trash*, she draws a rough line from the failed indentured servants of the sixteenth and seventeenth centuries to the squatters and tenant farmers of the eighteenth and nineteenth centuries and onward to the working poor of the twentieth. "We think of the left-behind groups as extinct, and the present as a time of advanced thought and sensibility," writes Isenberg. "But today's trailer trash are merely yesterday's vagrants on wheels, an updated version of Okies in

jalopies and Florida crackers in their carts." The American economy has always left someone behind, and the rest of us benefit
from the notion that the poor have only themselves to blame.

Even for those of us hanging on in the middle class, carrying the burden of hefty student loans and mortgage payments
and $6,375-per-capita credit card debt, what is our version of
the American Dream but an expanded vision of the indenture
system? With most of us clocking in each day to pad someone
else's pockets, we live paycheck-to-paycheck and save nothing for
retirement, let alone for our children.

And what about the true legacy of slavery? More qualified
writers than I have detailed the systematic oppression that the
descendants of slaves have faced since the end of the Civil War.
In "A Case for Reparations," Ta-Nehisi Coates summarizes it this
way: "Having been enslaved for 250 years, black people were not
left to their own devices. They were terrorized. In the Deep South,
a second slavery ruled. In the North, legislatures, mayors, civic
associations, banks, and citizens all colluded to pin black people
into ghettos, where they were overcrowded, overcharged, and
undereducated. Businesses discriminated against them, awarding
them the worst jobs and the worst wages. Police brutalized them
in the streets. And the notion that black lives, black bodies, and
black wealth were rightful targets remained deeply rooted in the
broader society."

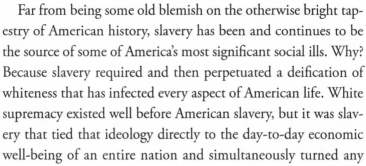

Far from being some old blemish on the otherwise bright tap-
estry of American history, slavery has been and continues to be
the source of some of America's most significant social ills. Why?
Because slavery required and then perpetuated a deification of
whiteness that has infected every aspect of American life. White
supremacy existed well before American slavery, but it was slavery that tied that ideology directly to the day-to-day economic
well-being of an entire nation and simultaneously turned any

Black progress into something dangerous. In this way slavery helped white America cultivate a grandiose vision of itself, and in the 150 years since the end of the Civil War, white America has persistently attempted to label Black America as inferior and then punished Black America for having the gall to try and prove things otherwise.

And yet, in spite of such opposition, there are millions of Black women and men in the United States today who've built successful lives and families. Many have genealogies not unlike my own, in that they've benefited from generations of parents sacrificing for their children and armies of supportive friends, neighbors, teachers, pastors, and other members of the community who've worked to help them succeed. The primary difference has been the role of race in that success. For generations of my family, race has worked for them; for generations of Black families, it has worked against them.

Scholars at the National Bureau of Economic Research recently used U.S. Census records, WWII draft records, and other sources to compare the intergenerational economic mobility of Black men between 1880 and 1990. Their basic question: How has race affected the ability of Black men to climb the social ladder? Part of their conclusion seems obvious, given America's racist disposition— "black sons have historically been significantly less likely than their white peers from similar economic backgrounds to ascend the income ladder," but a second conclusion is more striking: the systemic racism that contributes to these lower rates of economic mobility has "delayed the economic ascent of black men by a century." In other words, because white men like me have not faced generations of institutional racism, we have benefited, on average, from a one-hundred-year head start against our Black counterparts, economically speaking. One wonders, where might Black America be today if not for centuries of white oppression?

The legacies of indentured servitude and slavery are deeply entwined, and the relationship between class prejudice, racism, and struggle for social mobility might be summed up neatly in a line from Lyndon B. Johnson that Nancy Isenberg is fond of quoting: "If you can convince the lowest white man he's better than the best colored man, he won't notice you're picking his pocket. Hell, give him somebody to look down on, and he'll empty his pockets for you." Of course, for the average middle-class white person like me, it is easier to imagine success coming at the expense of individual hard work and resources than to accept that a social system based on racism and class prejudice may have given us some unfair advantages and a false sense of superiority to go with them. It's easier to see ourselves as the natural beneficiaries of an exacting but ultimately fair economy that we inherited from our indentured servant ancestors, rather than as stewards of a caste system based on centuries-old bigotry designed from the beginning to keep power in white, wealthy hands.

I think about my early ancestors a lot, about the trees they planted and the fields they plowed and the homes and barns and fences they built, the streams they diverted, and the endless early mornings they spent milking cows and tending herds; I think about the plains they walked and all their sacrifices that led down to me, and I wonder about the privileges I enjoy and which of them can be traced back to all the hard work that preceded me. I also think about the privileges they enjoyed as white European immigrants in eighteenth-century America. Theirs is a history of genuine frontier fortitude, and I've long held up that history as a model of simple faith, honest labor, and persistent hope. But frankly, without slave labor filling up work gangs on the large plantations, my immigrant ancestors literally would not have been free to purchase the open farmland of Pennsylvania; and without extensive land grabs that defrauded indigenous populations of millions of acres of territory, there wouldn't have been farmland for my ancestors to purchase anyway. Yes, their work ethic and cooperation helped their farms succeed, but it was their whiteness that gave that work ethic and cooperation real potential. And as the country grew and expanded, they continued to benefit from the intrinsic social trust that came from being white and moneyed. They could buy land, take out loans, and move freely. They could educate themselves, marry and amass wealth, and leave that wealth to their children. Of all the privileges I may have inherited, my skin color is the most obvious, if perhaps the least pleasant to acknowledge, but it's a combination of that whiteness and my middle-class heritage that has given such privilege its staying power.

I think about my parents too, and what they did for me to boost my social and cultural capital, and I can't help but think about my own sons and what I do for them, and the privilege I'm helping them maintain. We pay hundreds of dollars a month for sports leagues and music lessons and after-school programs. We visit museums and national parks and attend the theater and the symphony. We put them to work in the garden so they can learn the value of labor, and we give them weekly chores for the same reason. And just a few years ago, we did one of the most quintessentially white, middle-class things we've ever done: we moved across town to put the boys in better schools. Sure, I want them to chase the American Dream, but how to help them do that without also perpetuating notions of white supremacy and class superiority that are all but certainly germinating beneath the surface of their psyches right now. We tell our boys they can go anywhere and do anything and be anyone they want to be, but we don't talk enough about the unfair advantages they'll have simply by being white and middle class (not to mention male and Christian). They're growing up to be Swiss Army knives of privilege, and for all I'm doing to teach them the value of hard work, they must also understand that their country has too often valued race and class over everything else.

Today my parents live south of Salt Lake City in a well-manicured condo called The San Francisco. All the architecture mimics the famous painted ladies of the Bay City, and the buildings are divided up by small, well-groomed green spaces complete with curving paths and gurgling fountains. Every week, my mother takes her trash out the front door and carries it down the sidewalk to the dumpster (which she pays for), and in her kitchen the silverware rests neatly in a metal caddy on the counter. On bookshelves she has photos of her children, her grandchildren, and in two small oval frames, portraits of her parents. On one wall of the living room hangs a hand-tied quilt (a gift from Mom's sister) and above their fireplace a nineteenth-century cityscape in the Impressionist style. We visit every so often, crowding around their small dining room table, eating and telling stories while kids tinker on the piano and play with my parents' tiny dogs. And though the place is small, it feels homey, and after all those decades of watching Mom work so hard to accumulate so little, it's gratifying to see her so content in her own home, painting walls, hanging up her treasures, and building up a little equity. I find myself thinking, *If anyone deserves this, she does.* The entire place feels a bit redemptive, like a rationale for the ideal of the American Dream. I can almost hear James Truslow Adams. *Look what she's done for herself,* he might say. *Her own small kingdom, built up with her own two hands.*

And that oil painting above the fireplace is the centerpiece of the whole experience—pulling in colors from the walls and accents from around the room. The scene captures an evening in what I imagine is some anonymous colonial city, in a commercial part of town where working-class folks stroll in the moonlight just after an evening rainstorm. It might as well be a nod to our early-American roots and to the heritage of our hardworking immigrant ancestors, as much as a symbol of their sacrifices as my own mother's financial stability. But give the painting a closer look, and it also contains a slightly more menacing nod to history. Off to the side, tucked into the shrubbery is what looks like a makeshift homeless encampment, with tarpaulins strung between branches, sheets hung for privacy, and somewhere in the unseen darkness, are the poor, hiding in plain sight. And hidden even deeper, beneath the shadows of the city, built into the stone pavers and glimmering buildings and burning gas lamps, and emanating from the soil itself, is an economic system constructed largely on the backs of people of color. At first glance, you might not think of my mother's painting as an image that captures the complicated, contradictory history of the American Dream. But then, that's kind of the point of such nostalgic renderings of our colonial past. The image is a pleasant one, as long as you don't look too close.

Not in My Backyard

For a few months one summer when I was a kid, a man slept in the alleyway behind our home. Our backyard shared a fence with a two-story Methodist church that went largely unused during the week, and the small concrete patio beneath its back stairs made for a quiet, inviting shelter from the rain. The man generally came and went under the cover of night, so we didn't notice him much, but occasionally we'd hear him cough or smell cigarette smoke wafting over the fence, and we'd know he was back again. I don't remember actually fearing him, per se, but fearing the idea of him—the idea that someone could so easily breach our quiet suburban bubble. And I don't know how many nights he spent sleeping on the other side of our fence, but I do know that whenever we caught wind of him in our backyard, Dad would pick up the phone and call the police. I felt bad for the man on those nights, and I know Dad did too because after he hung up the phone, he always stuck his head out the window and hollered, in a not unkind voice, that the cops were coming, and he ought to get moving.

Twenty years on, and I found myself in Lubbock, Texas, with my own boys at a local children's festival held on the sprawling back lawn of the Mahon Public Library. We'd been coming to the library for several months, and the cozy children's section had begun to feel a little like home—its soft beanbag chairs and colorful posters, the endless pages of silly children's books, and the kind librarian who gave us stickers. On this day we were queued up for a giant inflatable castle when I noticed a rolled sleeping bag wedged in the branches of a tree a few feet away. Beside that tree, I saw two bedrolls perched in the limbs of a large juniper and, a few yards farther down, another sleeping bag tucked beneath some bushes. The boys' turn arrived, and as they jumped into the inflatable castle, I studied the faded fabric of a sleeping bag resting in the branches beside me, and I felt that same discomfort I'd felt years before when that homeless man showed up in our backyard. Only I couldn't help feeling that maybe this time, the intruder was me.

* * *

The pejorative label "NIMBY" is short for "Not in My Backyard" and is often applied to individuals in a community who support the building of prisons, landfills, and homeless shelters, as long as such development happens as far from their own interests as possible. "NIMBYs," as they are sometimes called, recognize the need to deal with social problems but don't see themselves as part of the solution. Let the problem be fixed, they say, but let someone else fix it. It is NIMBYism that shuffles homeless populations around cities, providing one short-term solution after another, and allows city councils, businesses, and neighborhood organizations to justify policies and practices aimed at "keeping neighborhoods safe," without addressing the reality of people living on the street. It is NIMBYism that feeds the false notion that we can do nothing ourselves and still expect the world to improve around us. In short, NIMBYism institutionalizes the idea that the correct response to a homeless man sleeping in the alley behind my home is not a blanket or a bowl of soup or even a call to the local shelter, but, rather, a call to the police.

* * *

After that library festival I asked around, and it turns out that for many years a rotating handful of transient individuals had been living on library grounds in Lubbock, taking advantage of the indoor air-conditioning by day and the warmth of the outdoor mechanical equipment by night. City leaders had long opposed any publicly funded shelter, but the Salvation Army and other ministries provided meals and limited bed space for those willing to accept a curfew and other rules. The library often became a resting spot for those who wanted to go it alone.

To address this situation, library administrators implemented a code of conduct with the stated purpose of maintaining "a safe, clean, and pleasant environment" for library guests. The policy prohibits, among other behaviors, panhandling; sleeping; bathing, shaving, and washing clothes in the bathrooms; leaving belongings unattended; and bringing bedrolls, luggage, or large plastic bags into the library. The policy also prohibits stinking or, as the document defines it, "bodily hygiene that is offensive so as to constitute a nuisance to other patrons," and it even bans certain types of mental illness, or, again in the document's words, "singing or talking to others or in monologues, or behaving in a manner which reasonably can be expected to disturb other persons."

Of course, such a response is to be expected from a busy urban library, so I'm not sure it's fair to judge them too severely. They are, after all, trying to serve the entire community, and the shelter and hygiene needs of the homeless population aren't actually part of a library's mission. And yet, I can hear buried in such policy language a slightly guilty conscience, the default response to homelessness that most of us embrace—a sheepish confession that wants to, but can't, for a variety of reasons, come out and say, "Homeless people make us all incredibly uncomfortable, so please stay out of sight so we can go back to ignoring the fact of your existence."

* * *

In Bremerton, Washington, a local developer planned to let a rescue mission build a temporary homeless camp on his land. The heated plywood shelters would give homeless individuals living in their cars a warmer, safer option for surviving long Washington winters. In addition to shelter, the site would include portable toilets, a fence, and a staff of volunteers. The developer brought a letter to his neighbors explaining his plan. "As we approach winter," he wrote, "there is the very real possibility a child may freeze to death in their car." He'd barely finished canvassing the neighborhood when protests erupted. Neighbors complained about safety, about property values, about the suddenness of the developer's plan, and about the lack of time to discuss or oppose the site. City commissioners expressed frustration with the developer for rushing things. There were calls for an environmental impact study. A local woman said the idea of a homeless encampment near her home made her "nauseous and queasy." "I haven't slept," she said.

In Akron, Ohio, city officials proposed an ordinance that would make it illegal to verbally ask for assistance within one hundred feet of an intersection. In Memphis, Tennessee, it's a misdemeanor to beg while sitting or leaning on a public bench. In Grand Rapids, Michigan, begging in public was flat out illegal until 2013. In Baltimore, Tampa Bay, Atlanta, Charlotte, Las Vegas, and dozens of other cities around the country, governments are trying to keep urban sidewalks and other public spaces welcoming to businesses and consumers while at the same time protecting the constitutional right of an individual to reach out for help. In many cities, current ordinances are slightly altered versions of older ones that have been struck down as unconstitutional. In Portland, Oregon, Mayor Sam Adams, speaking of his own third attempt at creating a "comprehensive sidewalk management plan," said to one reporter, "It's hard to legislate goodwill and common sense, but we're trying."

In Lubbock, just a few months after that library festival and, incidentally, just before one of the coldest Januarys on record, the city council placed a curfew on several downtown city properties, including the grounds of the Mahon Library. Anyone found loitering between midnight and 5:00 a.m. now faced up to $500 in fines. "Our city employees at the Mahon Library have to walk through unimaginable human waste [on] the way to work, dodging people in sleeping bags and all other manners of filth," said city councilman Paul Beane, inadvertently equating "people in sleeping bags" with "filth."

Within days of the curfew passing, nighttime temperatures dropped to single digits, and library regulars scrambled to locate shelter elsewhere. What a few of them found, with the help of local ministers who donated tents, was a patch of grass on the corner of Broadway and Avenue Q. The small park sat on a busy intersection near downtown but carried no restrictions on tents or overnight sleeping. Four men formalized the encampment by drafting a simple set of rules: no drinking, no drugs, and no fighting; and on January 10, 2011, Lubbock's Tent City was born.

In the lead-up to the curfew's passing, many Lubbock residents spoke out against the plan. Homelessness advocates argued that such a curfew would violate civil rights; local businesses worried the curfew would shift the homeless population onto their sidewalks; and a group of downtown residents expressed their own concerns: "We've got children and elderly," said one attendee. "What makes you think we're not going to be afraid?"

* * *

According to Desmond Morris, the concept of "stranger" is a relatively new one in the history of the human lexicon, and we have our cities to blame for it. "In the village, all the neighbours are personal friends," writes Morris. "Or, at worst, personal enemies." But in the modern urban city, we barely know anyone's name. If someone finds Grandpa sitting on the ground, hungry and cold in the village market, everyone stops to help. But in the city, Grandpa devolves into "some old man." At best we figure someone else will help him out, and at worst, we don't even see him. This is an actual physiological phenomenon. The social cognition portion of our brains that is supposed to help us recognize other human beings—it often fails to "light up" when confronted with someone who appears to be homeless. Socioneurologists call this neural blindness, and it may help explain why it is so difficult for civil society to think about the homelessness issue in terms other than public safety, commercial impact, property rights, and the smell of urine. We can't treat one another humanely if we don't, at the outset, see one another as human.

* * *

The first homeless person I met in Lubbock was a man named Joe, a thirty-six-year-old army vet with a penchant for cut-off T-shirts and washed-out Wranglers. He smelled aggressively of body odor and cigarettes, and his teeth were crooked and encrusted with plaque. He'd spent most of his adult life outside, living for some time on a beach in Florida after dropping out of high school and then enlisting for a few years in the military before getting discharged for fighting. He then bounced from one construction job to another, never earning enough money to get a permanent place of his own or put down any roots at all. When I met him in the late winter of 2011, Joe and his wife, Melissa, had recently arrived in Lubbock on a one-way Greyhound ticket. Joe was on probation, and they were looking for a fresh start. They ended up at Tent City.

I met Joe and Melissa through a local street preacher named Tinker Carlen—a large man in his eighties who got around with the help of a medical scooter and wore an oxygen line attached to a silver tank he carried with him. Tinker spoke with a slur, and the oxygen line added a bit of nasal distortion to his otherwise deep, buttery voice. He'd once played guitar with Buddy Holly and the Crickets, but he'd spent the last fifty years in various forms of street ministry. He lived just up the road from me in a semidilapidated ranch home with an overgrown backyard littered with upturned lawn furniture, old car parts, and other odd junk. I'd stopped in to see him one afternoon, and Joe and Melissa were sitting on his couch.

"These here are good people," Tinker had said, and he told me the story of how they'd met. He'd gone down to Tent City with a hundred dollars to give away. "I asked Joe to take the money to a convenience store and buy some cigarettes for everyone," said Tinker. If Joe came back with cigarettes and change, Tinker knew he could trust him. And that's exactly what happened. "I invited Joe and Melissa to live in my spare room," he said, gesturing down the hall. "You know, help them get a leg up." I tried to imagine Tinker cruising the encampment in his motorized chair, one hundred dollars in his hand, looking to give away a miracle. "When I was young I used to pray for God to give me a church," Tinker said on more than one occasion. "I woke up one day and realized the Lord had given me the street—the biggest church of all."

The following Sunday Joe and Melissa came out to church with me, and my bishop asked me to help them out—give Joe rides to meet his probation officer, take them to the grocery store with a check from the church, help them with job applications and Melissa's disability claim. I paid Joe to fix my car a couple of times, found him a few odd jobs, and invited them both over for the occasional dinner. Once, while we were replacing spark plugs in my driveway, I asked Joe about coming to Lubbock and staying at Tent City. He told me the place had given him a bit of hope. He and Melissa had somewhere to stay, and on Sundays they could make a little money selling the local newspaper on street corners. "Too many places look at you like you're less than human," he told me. "At Tent City, I could just be myself."

* * *

City officials in Lubbock might have tolerated Tent City longer if its founders had chosen a less conspicuous location. The campers weren't breaking any laws, but they were, as one member of the city council put it, making things "complicated" for surrounding businesses. "There are people flying in to sign contracts with these buildings, and they are leaving," said Councilwoman Gibson. "It has nothing to do with the people that live there. But we're also losing opportunities for jobs coming into Lubbock." The parks department expressed its own concerns—spring was just around the corner, and all those tents and people would make lawn care a hassle.

A donor offered land in a heavy industrial zone on the east end of downtown—far from commercial interests, suburban shoppers, and anxious members of the city council—a new home for the homeless, largely out of sight, literally on the other side of the tracks. The city council had no objections, so Tent City residents pulled stakes and moved across town.

* * *

In the last weeks of winter that year, three homeless men were brought to the university hospital with crippling frostbite, their legs blackened and dead below the knees. "I cut off three sets of legs in one day," said an orthopedic surgeon who'd been on call that day. "It was pretty easy to count back the weeks to the cold snap in January." At the end of his shift, he told me, he and his supervisor had sat talking about the men. "Perhaps I ought to make copies of their bills," said the supervisor, "and send it to the city council." By his calculation, the total cost for the amputation, hospital recovery, and a lifetime of prosthesis would reach into the hundreds of thousands of dollars. It might be more cost effective, he pointed out, to just build a shelter.

A short time later, a large dust storm blew through Lubbock. Seventy-mile-per-hour gusts came down from the northwest, kicking dirt into the air as high as eight thousand feet and smothering the region in a brown fog that stretched nearly one hundred miles to the New Mexico border. The storm snapped tree limbs and downed power lines, which then sparked three different wildfires. Traffic in the city stopped, and pedestrians ran for cover as the storm cut visibility to almost zero. At Tent City's new location, some residents took cover in a common building. Others were caught out in their tents, most of which were blown down and broken. Rick Burrow, a Tent City resident away from the encampment, took shelter at a Walmart. On a local news site, beneath an article about the storm, a minor debate broke out. Most commenters were sympathetic and supportive, but one commenter wrote, "I wonder if Mr. Burrow bothered to apply for a job while squatting out the storm at Wal-Mart." and another saw the storm as a sign from heaven. "These people at Tent City are alcoholics and drug addicts. VERY VERY few exceptions," wrote the author of the anonymous post. "They put themselves where they are. Let this be a lesson to others . . . the wages of sin is death!"

* * *

Once a week or so that spring, I stopped by Tinker's house to see how things were going. Joe and Melissa cleaned the kitchen and washed Tinker's car; they took care of the yard and prepared food. They reminded Tinker to take his medicine, helped rub ointment into the sores on his arms and legs, and monitored his oxygen tank, keeping the lines clean and ensuring the tank didn't run out. In exchange Tinker let them sleep in a back room, and he did the grocery shopping and paid the bills. Their friends back at Tent City thought that Joe and Melissa had won the lottery, and whenever I spoke with them, they were effusive about Tinker's generosity.

The problem? Tinker's family apparently didn't like the situation. Joe was rough and big—not tall but thick, maybe 250 pounds— and he had crooked teeth and neck tattoos—an anarchist's A and the phrase "mi vida loca" across the base of his skull. He wore steel-toed boots that he called "shit kickers," and when asked about the Confederate flag he liked to display, he would shrug. "It's heritage, not hate." He'd spent time in jail for killing a dog (he described it as putting a sick animal out of its misery), and he'd once tried to pry out his own rotten tooth with a kitchen spoon. Melissa suffered from a potent mixture of anxiety and excitability that, according to Joe, made her unpredictable in a group and a potential danger to herself if she spent too much time alone.

Together Joe and Melissa were always grateful for help and they were generous with everyone around them, but they bathed and washed their clothes only occasionally, and they ate ferociously—I remember watching Joe eat three peanut butter and jelly sandwiches at once, all stacked on top of one another, and on more than one occasion I witnessed Melissa eat an entire half-pound block of cheese, one large mouthful after another, as if it were a candy bar.

All this was, I suppose, too much for Tinker's adult children. I never spoke with them, but Joe told me that Tinker's family was worried about the sort of people their father had invited into his home—these freeloading strangers driving his car, eating his food, and poking around his medical equipment—who knew what their intentions were? Could they be trusted? Were they the sorts of people Tinker's money should be going to? I imagine they had all the same questions I would if my father had let strangers move in off the street and into his spare bedroom. By the end of the summer, Tinker's family had convinced him that Joe and Melissa were too big a risk, and they would have to go.

* * *

Churches, street gangs, book clubs, the NRA, even family—these groups fulfill a basic human need to belong. They also fulfill a basic human desire to draw distinctions, to put up fences, to relieve some of the burden of responsibility that we naturally feel for one another. There's no doubt that we are our brothers' keepers. The real question is, who are our brothers? And the fact that "everyone" is both the correct answer and the one we don't want to hear is less an indictment of humanity and more an acknowledgment of the difficult tightrope we walk as compassionate, spiritual beings who also happen to be higher-order mammals who occasionally struggle to shake that instinct to eat the weakest in the litter.

* * *

Tent City hadn't been at its new location a month when once again concerns started pouring in from nearby property owners. There were all the usual anxieties—suppositions about crime rates and property values—but this time someone got in touch with the city's Planning and Zoning Commission. Apparently Tent City's donated lot wasn't zoned for temporary shelters, and Tent City leadership would have to apply to get the zoning changed. Either that or find a new home, again.

"It's infuriating," said one Tent City administrator. "An organization stepped up to the plate, and we brought them out here to private property . . . now they want us to move them somewhere else."

In the end, citing the "overwhelming opposition of businesses," the Planning and Zoning Commission voted seven to zero, with one abstention, to reject Tent City's request for rezoning, which, according to Councilman Paul Beane, was no real surprise: "I don't think anybody in their right mind ever thought the tent city was going to be a permanent solution."

Tent City's last hope was a direct appeal to the city council. An email petition collected more than 2,600 signatures, and invitations to attend the hearing went out via email and Facebook. Joe and I decided to attend the meeting together, which was set for the morning of October 27, 2011. We arrived just before 7:30 a.m. and joined a standing-room-only crowd listening to the hearing from the foyer of the building.

One by one, the council members spoke of the progress the community had made in helping the homeless, of their desire to find a solution to the short-term housing needs in the city, and of their belief that Tent City should be given more time to become that solution. Several members of the audience spoke, but the atmosphere was anticlimactic. Everyone talked as if overturning the Planning and Zoning Commission's decision was a foregone conclusion, and, in the end, it was. The council members present voted unanimously to grant Tent City a thirty-month probationary period in which to establish the viability of the shelter.

Chuck Chapman, one of the neighboring property owners who had originally complained about Tent City, had a change of heart after talking with shelter administrators: "The bottom line is, I know nobody wants it," he told reporters. "But me, my partner, and my building—we are willing to have it in our backyard."

* * *

When Joe and Melissa were asked to leave Tinker's home, our congregation put them up in an apartment down the street. Folks from church donated an old couch and a bed, a television and a kitchen table, a few pots and pans, some dishes and silverware, and a coffee table. The plan was to cover their rent until they could get steady work, and Joe and Melissa were thrilled to have a place of their own. Joe talked big plans about starting his lawn-care business or maybe getting his commercial driver's license. Their Tent City friends thought Joe and Melissa had hit the jackpot for a second time.

Once or twice a week I came by their apartment to take them shopping and check on their employment progress. And though there were signs that the whole plan might fall apart within a few months, at the time it all seemed rather foolproof. With an address to call their own, they were one Laundromat run and a warm shower away from being ready to enter the workforce. How hard could this be?

Because both Joe and Melissa had managed at Tinker's so well, I assumed they would embrace the domestic life we'd placed them in, but after just a few weeks, it became clear that they were going to need more significant interventions than we could provide. They needed training in everything from housekeeping and grocery shopping to job hunting and interview skills. Each week we'd make a menu and hit the aisles of the grocery store together, filling the cart as a team—meat, cheese, bread, and eggs, but also Mountain Dew, Fruit Loops, ice cream, and cookies. I'd help them load their fridge on a Saturday afternoon, and in a week's time I'd come back to find all the soda, cereal, and peanut butter gone, but produce wilting in the crisper, meat souring in its cellophane, and a few half-eaten meals fermenting in their day-old pots.

I took them once to the local employment office and sat with Joe at a computer and scrolled through employment advertisements. I figured we'd print out some applications, make some phone calls, and set up some interviews. Instead we stared at the screen, and Joe got frustrated. He told me about all the jobs that had come and gone. About the bosses that had mistreated him. He grew visibly uncomfortable at the prospect of paperwork or phone calls. He took the applications I printed off for him and never filled them out. I'd see him later that week standing on a street corner, holding a cardboard sign.

At their apartment the dishes and laundry piled up from week to week, and their floor grew so cluttered that I had to clear a path with my feet just to make it across the room. One Saturday afternoon when I stopped by to check on them, Joe told me, in a rather embarrassed voice, that they were out of toilet paper. It had been days, and he hadn't told me. I asked him how they'd managed, and he told me, pointing to a black plastic bag tied up in the corner, "Well, I've got a lot of old T-shirts."

They found a cat, but it got stuck under the fridge and died. They got a dog for free out of the paper, but it fell ill, and it died as well. They landed a series of short-term roommates who I often found sleeping on the couch when I came to visit. They'd stay a few days, eat up extra food, and disappear. Joe found odd jobs hauling steel or laying carpets at a local hotel, but the work was under the table, and he rarely got paid. Week in and week out, this is how their life went. And I don't mention any of this to be critical. But rather to point out how little I understood the challenges that Joe and Melissa faced, and how clueless I was as to the kind of help they really needed.

* * *

In the modern world, write Eric Kramer and Soobum Lee, a person is valuable only if they are exploitable. "Dysfunctional individuals are worthless," they write. "They are 'nobodies.' . . . They cannot secure a place, a 'position,' within the socioeconomic structure. They have no identity. They literally have nowhere to go." And this gets back to the question at hand—if a certain segment of the population faces serious roadblocks on the way to managing their own physical, emotional, or psychological fitness, what is to be done? Tinker wanted to give Joe and Melissa a "leg up." When my bishop assigned me to work with them, he told me the same thing, in not so many words. All three of us were operating under the bootstrap assumption that given the right set of opportunities, anyone can become an independent, functioning member of society. But what if Tinker, my bishop, and I are wrong about such assumptions? Sure, all I need is the opportunity and I'll go to school, get a job, save for a down payment. But I grew up in the privilege of the normative middle class. How might the realm of possibility change for an adult who has spent twenty years living on the street? And what if two decades on the street is compounded by mental illness or addiction? Moreover, what if "independence" and "functionality" are not necessarily the ideals we think they are? Or rather, what if such ideals are actually just a means to another cynical end—the shortest "humane" route to getting that homeless person out of my sight so I can go on with my life and still feel okay when I go to bed each night?

* * *

One morning in late summer Joe and I made plans to go to the employment office, but when I went to pick him up, he wasn't home. I caught up with him by phone, and he told me he was out with friends and wouldn't make it. The next day, though, Joe called me back and told me the real story. His brother had come to town from Mississippi, and they'd all decided to head back home together—they were, right then, on the road. I heard in Joe's voice something that sounded like regret as he apologized for leaving us the mess in his apartment, and then he thanked me for all my help and hung up. That afternoon, with some other men from our church, I cleaned out their apartment, trash by the bagful, pots of food cold on the stove, so much detritus on the carpet that we had to use rakes and shovels to scrape it up and bag it for disposal. We hauled the couch and the table to the curb, dumpstered the mattress and bags of garbage, and wiped down counters as best we could. And when I left that night, I felt both sad that Joe and Melissa had decided to go and also a little relieved that they were finally gone.

* * *

While looking through the online archives of local newspapers and television stations in Lubbock, I came across a picture of Joe and Melissa, published alongside an article about Tent City's forced move. The picture was taken before I'd known them and their story. The photo shows Joe sitting and resting his head against Melissa, who is partially cropped out of the picture. Joe's eyes are closed, and he looks a little haggard. "We're not a bunch of mindless animals," Joe told the reporter. "We are just like everybody else." In my mind I could hear Joe's deep country drawl and imagine the way he swung his hands when he talked. If I had never met Joe or Melissa, that photo in the archive would have meant very little—just another set of problems for someone else to deal with. But I do know them. We've shared meals and jokes, and I've washed their dishes and swept their kitchen floor. And so it isn't easy to click away from the page when they're staring at me from that screen. In all my own frenzied focus on accumulating things and feeding my own, Joe and Melissa remind me that I am capable of other ways of seeing. Of course, I have to feed my own—and there are real limits to what I can do to help, but compassion does not strike me as something meant to be rationed.

* * *

In the years since I left Lubbock, Tent City has become a permanent fixture downtown. Local high school students have helped put up a fence and new canvas tents, and a large outbuilding has been insulated and converted into a common area with tables, couches, and a television. School groups have donated clothing, food, and labor, and Texas Tech's business school installed solar panels that provide lighting and electricity in each tent. Just recently, a nonprofit organization called Paul's Project took over management of Tent City and renamed it Grace Campus. Paul's Project has long-term plans that include replacing tents with tiny homes and offering classes in anger management, addiction recovery, and job skills. In the past year, Paul's Project has helped more than one thousand people in Lubbock with everything from transitional housing and emergency shelter to job placement and counseling.

Looking at Lubbock's progress, I'm reminded again of Councilman Beane's comment about how "no one in their right mind ever thought the tent city was going to be a permanent solution." And I think he may have been correct, if by "right mind" he meant typical, average, or predictable. But what Lubbock seems to be proving is that despite the persistent ambivalence of government entities, and in the face of the collective fears of a community, individuals can defy their own biological proclivities and social insecurities and do something to make a city feel a little more like a village.

* * *

My thoughts often return to that man who spent those weeks one summer sleeping in the alley behind my home and to what my family and I could have but didn't do for him. I doubt he ever came two nights in a row, but I imagine the stairs were a regular stop on his circuit of our semi-suburban neighborhood of old houses, small storefronts, and quiet churches. He must have stopped smoking, at least behind our house, because as time went on, it became more difficult to tell when he was around. In fact, we probably never would have noticed him once the smoke disappeared if he hadn't suffered from such a rasping cough. Sometimes weeks would go by without any sign of him, and then one night I would be standing in our kitchen with the window open, and I would hear his cough betray him through the silent evening. And finally, when months had passed without hearing him, I knew he had opened a seam in the darkness and disappeared into the night forever.

Today I wonder what part of our home betrayed itself to that man haunting the patio under those stairs: the ringing of a phone, the clank of dishes in the sink, the chuckles and tears and slammed doors of a typical family home? Were we anything more than just another house of "haves" laughing on the other side of the fence? Did he wish we'd shut our windows? Did he wish we'd turn out the porch light so he could sleep? Did he turn up his collar against the cold and try to pretend we weren't even there?

Thursday Night Lights

Late September, one of the first few games of the junior varsity season, and the sunlight shimmered over the field in a mother-of-pearl sunset. A scene that might have taken my breath away if I hadn't been quivering at the line of scrimmage, distracted by the preternaturally muscular defensive end across from me who was, at that moment, stomping the ground like an angry bull and growling out epithets about my mother and how he was going to eat me alive. Those weren't his exact words, but they capture the gist of the moment. Whereas he appeared to have embraced the barbarian football player cliché right down to the guttural animal noises and war-paint smears of eye black on each cheek, I was kneeling there in a uniform that smelled like fabric softener, trying not to cry. I'd just been called for my second false start in as many plays, which means I'd cost the team ten yards and given my barbarian counterpart ample opportunity to review with me what would happen if I managed to hold my ground and let the play commence as my irritated quarterback intended. In the barbarian's assessment, I was about to experience significant discomfort, as he told me repeatedly that he and his fellow defensive linemen were going to "bring the pain"; that he in particular was going to "walk all over" me; and, perhaps most surprisingly, my "ass," he kept on saying, was his, and it was going to be his "all day."

And he kept repeating that line with animal intensity: "All day; all day," he kept saying, broken up by a few expletives that don't warrant repeating here. This young man also wanted to know if I was "ready" for him, which I think was a rhetorical question because if the two false-start penalties revealed anything, it was my lack of preparation for just this sort of moment.

Let me pause here briefly, before the climax of this epic sports memory, and tell you that I volunteered for this nonsense, that this was my second year playing football for my high school, and that I was a first-string junior varsity athlete on both offense and defense. I mention this not to boast, since the basic requirement for a starting position on our JV football team was a heartbeat and the ability to breathe through a mouthpiece, but rather to explain how I got into this situation in the first place. Football is a no-cut sport, which means in a big high school like mine, a single team could have upward of sixty players, and the entire program served as a catch-all for a wide variety of teenage boys who joined up for all kinds of reasons, only a few of which had to do with a love for the game.

Some boys suited up because their older brothers did, like my friend Tommy, whose beefy brother had been a star years before on the varsity squad. For others the choice was oedipal. My friend Kyle was the youngest and smallest son in his family, and his dad was the varsity head coach.

Rumor had it that Kyle took football so seriously that he'd agreed to redo the eighth grade to give himself an extra year to bulk up—if that were true, then he'd effectively red-shirted his freshman year of high school. Then there's the group of players we'll call cheerleader groupies—boys who join the team because of their faith in the social cachet of football, convinced that a few years in oversized pads will make an impression on the hearts and minds of the slender ladies holding the pom-poms, or, if not on them, then on some other girl in the stands. In addition to all these, every team invariably hosts a group of kids who play because their fathers make them and another group who play because puberty hit them hard, and they morphed into burly boy-men too big for basketball or other sports.

Add to this list boys with nothing better to do, boys who play because their friends play, a few boys who grew up genuinely loving the game, and, of course, the small gang of boys with an actual future in the sport—winners of the genetic lottery who play because they seemed preordained by God to do so, regardless of whether they actually want to or not. Put all these factions together on one field and throw them into matching uniforms and you have your typical junior varsity football team. *Ragtag* is a word. *Ridiculous* is another.

In the locker room before games we blasted Metallica and put athletic tape around our hands and thighs because we thought we'd seen the older boys do something similar. While we waited for practice to start, some of us slept on the benches, others played catch, and others snapped towels and roughhoused until one day someone decided it would be fun to take turns making each other pass out in the empty shower stalls. That's the image that stays with me from high school football. Half-dressed teenage boys giggling as they watch one of their own press their hands against the neck of a two-hundred-pound fourteen-year-old until his face turns red, then blue, and then his eyes roll, and he falls to the tile floor; cheers would erupt when he came to, and everyone had a good laugh.

In our team photo we're all lined up on the bleachers doing our best to look tough, but the devil is in the details. Front and center are all the specimen athletes, future varsity stars who fill out their pads with purpose, muscular teenagers who not only play every down of our Thursday afternoon games, but even play a few downs every Friday night on the varsity team, getting in extra reps to prepare them for their inevitable rise through the ranks. These are the players that would make cheerleaders swoon, if cheerleaders came to JV games.

Along the back rows and outer edges of the photograph are the rest of us: a fourth-string receiver with flamingo knees and chicken-bone shoulders buried beneath a set of pads two sizes too large, a six-foot-three behemoth of a boy who ran like his legs had just been introduced to his body, and next to them a kid who'd played Pop Warner ball all through middle school and would have been a halfway decent quarterback if he hadn't started smoking weed behind the school gym almost every afternoon. And in between them all, dozens of anonymous boys—unpaid extras in this teenage theater of the absurd, all of us depressingly average in our speed and agility, destined for futures in finance, dentistry, retail management, and elastic waistbands. These were my people.

At fifteen years old, I stood six feet tall, if I wore my thick cleats, and I weighed about 150 pounds with all my gear on. If you saw me in my pads from a distance, you could easily mistake me for one of at least twenty other boys on the team. Sure, I could run up and down the field without passing out, but I could catch a ball only about half the time, and I'd most certainly stopped growing, so at best I had potential as a second-string utility player who'd take nothing with him when he graduated but bad knees and the chorus to "Enter Sandman" permanently engrained in his memory.

Then why play at all, you might ask. My older brother played, but only one year, and my dad thought playing was a great idea, but he never pressured me to sign up, so family legacy wasn't really the issue. I definitely bought into the idea that football raised my chances with girls, if only a little, and I'm sure I entertained the notion that I'd look pretty great wearing my uniform to school on game days the way varsity players did. But really, I was a member of the "My friends are playing, so why not" club. Tommy and Kyle were on the list from the day they were born, and my other best friend at the time—Isaiah—his dad had played for the New Orleans Saints, so we knew he was going to play. Hanging out that summer before high school, our conversations turned to football almost every day; by August they'd worn me down, and I agreed to sign up.

And that brings us to our present scene on a bright Oregon afternoon in September, with me staring up from my crouched position at a rabid teenager, who, from behind his metal face-mask, looked genuinely determined to hurt me. I imagine that watching me cowering there across from him, he could see quite clearly that I had no business being on that football field. If he only knew the whole truth—that I had no threshold for pain, and certainly had no interest in inflicting it on others; that when it came to aggression, I had the constitution of a sheared lamb; that if I ever managed a halfway decent tackle, I always helped the guy up afterward and even apologized if I thought I'd hit him too hard; that while other guys considered their filthy practice jerseys a badge of honor and kept them unwashed in their lockers the whole season, I took mine home every night to put through the laundry and brought them back, folded and neat each after-noon; that while other boys were making each other pass out in the shower room, I was working on homework; that the tears in my eyes at that moment were neither the first, nor the last that I would shed beneath my helmet; that if he'd asked, I couldn't explain those tears except to say something about shame and the distinct impression that football was supposed to turn me into a man and that the project was failing miserably.

Of course, he wouldn't ask, but perhaps we both would have been better off if we'd had the chance to explain ourselves—a little "talk-it-out" session right there on the forty-yard line. He might ask me about my tears and why I'd signed up to play in the first place, and I might ask about his performance of all that stomping and rough language and who it was for, anyway. His teammates? His coaches? His father in the stands? Maybe some girl? Or was it really just for me? A pissing contest that he was clearly winning? Or maybe the same fears and worries that manifested in me as tears and quivering, manifested in him as chest thumping and trash talk about my mom.

But this was no place for such questions—facing off in a JV football game on a Thursday afternoon in front of a dozen casually interested parents and fans on a poorly marked field under the fading light of an autumn afternoon. So instead I set my teeth, determined this time to hold my position, whatever foot-stomping verbal abuse might come my way, and I waited. The only certain method for avoiding a false start in football is to let the other guy hit you first, so that's what I did. I crouched there on the ground, vision blurred by tears, mind swirling with the barbarian's insults and the disappointed voices of my teammates (who, just moments before during the huddle had offered their own assessment of my performance), and I waited for the pop of his pads against mine.

The cadence came from the quarterback, the center snapped the ball, and at once the barbarian was on me; I jammed my hands into his chest just underneath his shoulder pads, and, leveraging his momentum, drove him toward the sidelines. This was no graceful football move—more like a Thelma and Louise act of desperation, except we weren't heading for the edge of a cliff, but to the white chalk at the edge of the field. And if there hadn't been a sideline, if there hadn't been a referee somewhere blowing his whistle, if my motley team hadn't been waiting for me back in the huddle, I might have kept on running, right off the field and into that mother-of-pearl sunset.

The Full Montaigne

> If I had lived among those nations, which (they say) yet dwell under
> the sweet liberty of nature's primitive laws, I assure thee I would
> most willingly have painted myself quite fully and quite naked.
> —MICHEL DE MONTAIGNE, "To the Reader"

One comes to expect certain familiar images on a morning commute from the suburbs—rows of sleepy houses, the occasional
early-morning jogger, newspapers resting on driveways like Tic Tacs
on the tongue, a garbage truck maybe, or the long glow of school
bus lights lumbering through the neighborhood. One might even
expect three or four semitrucks parked along the main road, if
one lives, as I do, around the corner from a busy truck stop off the
freeway. But even here where the suburbs give way to the bustle of
the interstate corridor, no one expects to look up into the cab of
one of those trucks and see a three-hundred-pound man standing
there in the morning light, naked as the day is long. But if you happen to suffer from such impeccable timing, as I did one morning
a few months ago, you might have trouble shaking the image of
that man's ample buttocks, glinting, as they were, in the rising sun.

For most of us, the nakedness of strangers—not the stuff of magazine covers or celluloid sex scenes, but real nakedness—isn't

something we encounter much outside the locker room at the gym. And for most of us, that's more than enough. I've made a study of keeping my head down as I slip out of my jeans and into a pair of trunks, keeping my towel about me as I drop my drawers, and keeping my gaze fixed on the locker in front of me as I talk with a changing friend at my side—all essential doctrines in the golden rule of unavoidable public nudity. But I'm confounded by the old men of the locker room with their dazzling confidence and disheveled hair, their sun-starved backs and spotted legs, their stately weight gain and the stiffness in their steps as they stride from locker to sink, naked but for the towels draped over their shoulders. There's something to envy in the way these men queue up at the sink and wash their hands or wring out their swimsuits or simply stand there, arms raised in gesture like some marbled tribute to geriatric vitality. I don't think I'll ever feel that comfortable in my own skin.

Emmanuel Levinas writes that nakedness is the root cause of shame, but not in the way you might think. Sure, most of us are mortified by the thought of public nudity, but, says Levinas, "The fault consists not in the lack of propriety, but almost in the very fact of having a body, of being there." Pure shame, it seems, is less about how others might see us, and more about how we see ourselves.

The first man I ever saw naked had to be my father, though I have no recollection of such a first, only an image—Dad as one of those old titans of the locker room walking down our hallway, startling in his bare-bottom bravado. He seemed always to forget something on his way to the shower—a razor, a washcloth, a bar of soap—and if my sister wasn't home, he would emerge from his room without a stitch of clothing or an ounce of shame. Dad served in the navy and then as a police officer in Washington DC, and it showed in the conviction of his stride—he was a man on a mission, and if you happened to be caught in his path you could do little but press yourself against the wall, mortified, and avert your eyes.

Mortification: literally "to kill," though it occasionally refers to the strict discipline of the spirit over the body—John the Baptist in his hair shirt, my Muslim friend on his Ramadan fast, the Jain monk in his quiet nakedness. But death still lives within these notions of self-flagellation, the spirit defeating the body and leaving it behind, as if we could ever really escape ourselves. Even when mortification merely means "embarrassment," there's still a sense of what Levinas was getting at—this nausea over our own existence, this need to rid ourselves of ourselves. To say one might "die from shame" is not so much a statement of fear, but of desperate desire.

* * *

Montaigne, first prophet of the essay, hoped his work would channel a certain "genuine, simple, and ordinary manner, without study and artifice," and he assures us that had propriety not forbidden him, he would have written himself "quite fully and quite naked." And while such a statement can't help but sound a little cheeky, I appreciate its stress on an essayist's need to strip down. What is to be done, after all, with the realization that we are, as Levinas put it, "riveted" to ourselves? Perhaps the confiding exhibitionism of the essay is an attempt to mitigate our shame. If I am genuine, simple, and ordinary on the page, the essayist seems to say, then perhaps that might make up for who I am the rest of the time.

We weren't a family prone to exhibitionism, but Dad had a bit of a body temperature regulation problem and didn't work much, which meant aside from stalking naked down the hall every so often, he spent a lot of time sitting around the house in what he affectionately called his "skivvies." So much time, in fact, that when any of us brought a friend over, the first thing we did was open the front door and holler, "Everybody decent?" We meant "dressed" of course, and the question was a legitimate one. Walking in on Dad in his underwear was an initiation of sorts—you weren't a real friend until you'd seen my half-naked father dart from the family room and heard his astonished apology from behind a closed door, as if three o'clock in the afternoon were a perfectly reasonable time to take off one's pants for the day. I remember this as mildly embarrassing but also empowering. All teenagers need a reason to feel superior to their parents, and not spending my afternoons reading the newspaper in my underwear was an easy bar to clear.

I have three boys, and with the melodrama of their teenage years all but upon us, I'm sometimes overwhelmed by how much they all still have to learn. We call it "Owning a Body 101" at our house, and the curriculum covers everything from chewing with one's mouth closed to lifting the seat and flushing the toilet. When they were younger, this meant daily reminders that "our bodies are private." And yet, when bath time would come around, they had no qualms about dropping their pants in the living room, and after bath time they'd run naked laps around the kitchen with their towels fluttering behind them. In the pool locker room I'd field questions about all my inexplicable body hair, and if Ian, our youngest boy, happened to walk in on one of his older brothers stepping out of the shower, it wasn't uncommon to hear him yell, "I see your penis!"

Now that they're older, though, we've moved on to more serious matters—farting in public and wiping our snot on our sleeves and taking the last slice of chocolate cake and failing to comb our hair or tuck in our shirt and picking scabs and refusing to take showers and forgetting to put on deodorant despite three separate reminders from Dad in one morning. At times my boys can be walking time bombs of cringe-worthy social impropriety, and sometimes I want to duct-tape their mouths shut when we're out in public. This doesn't make them bad kids, I know, but I'm sometimes at a loss for what to do with their obliviousness to the social conventions that I've spent the better part of a decade trying to teach them. And I'm talking about more than simple matters of decorum. These first lessons in owning a body seem like groundwork for the self-awareness they'll need when those bodies begin to develop minds of their own, when testosterone and social pressure and Freud will begin to complicate everything, when their own reflection will begin to look like a stranger. Despite my apprehension though, I suppose a part of me is simply jealous. Sure, each of my boys knows he has a body, but they haven't yet learned to despise them.

Montaigne's only surviving daughter was barely three years old in 1574 when he wrote "On the Custom of Wearing Clothes," and though he does not mention little Léonor dashing naked through the halls after bath time at the Chateau de Montaigne, I can imagine such an image inspiring the essay's claim that naked-ness is "the original fashion of mankind." To Montaigne, it was unimaginable that among all earth's creatures humans alone might be ill-equipped to survive the natural world. He catalogs the rel-ative nakedness of Turkish esthetes, of soldiers on the battlefield, and of a local peasant who, when asked how he survives the cold in just his shirt sleeves, replied, "Sir, you go with your face bare:

I am all face." And if there's a lesson in this catalog of nakedness, perhaps it resides in this peasant's shameless optimism—a kind of clear-headed self-consciousness that allows him to see his own nakedness without seeing it as a liability. Such self-mastery just might top the list of our greatest adaptations for survival.

* * *

I remember as a child wanting to hide the fact of my parents— especially my father who excelled in all the usual ways of embarrassing his children. He drove a series of beat-up old cars, worked intermittently at thankless, low-paying jobs, and asked my friends awkward questions about their love lives. His specialties, though, have always been the lame joke and the protracted story. He has jokes about "my old girlfriend" who "really enjoyed her job at the auto shop pulling off hubcaps with her teeth"—the same girl who had to "wear high heels to keep her knuckles from dragging on the ground" and who was "so ugly we had to tie a pork chop around her neck so the dog would play with her." He has a series of jokes about elephants hiding in the refrigerator and leaving footprints in the Jell-O and a set about elephants giving alligators flat noses by jumping out of trees in the jungle. There's a joke about a cow with two legs (lean beef), and a cow with no legs (ground beef), and another dozen or so that don't come to mind that he picked up from late-night television, from his days in the navy, from *Reader's Digest*, jokes he puts on like some gaudy robe to parade around the neighborhood.

And his stories have served much the same purpose. He name-drops about his time as a stage guard for Elvis in Las Vegas, the time he arrested Sonny Liston, the time he worked on Capitol Hill for a Nevada senator, the time he helped bring down a Las Vegas conman. He has real estate stories about big sales and seedy agents and navy stories about flying around the North Atlantic in the glass nose of a P-2 Neptune. To the uninitiated, Dad's stories and jokes suggest confidence and wit, but to those of us who know him, his old yarns feel like little more than diversion tactics, stories to hide the self-conscious man beneath the surface—jokes to make us all laugh, I suppose, and eliminate the possibility of anyone laughing at him.

In high school, I never could get used to looking in the mirror. I'd stare at myself and wonder, where did these arms come from? These meaty thighs, these bushy eyebrows? And I felt as awkward with language as I did with my own body. It seemed that no matter what came out of my mouth, it all devolved into bluster and poorly timed humor that rarely said anything more than "I'm trying too hard." I felt always on the verge of molting another layer, as if the real me was still waiting somewhere beneath the surface. I felt perpetually undercooked, partially formed, and unready for public consumption.

It never occurred to me that a grown man could feel the same way—that it might be some kind of mutated teenage angst that so often kept my father at home in his underwear, or else out, but dressed in old stories and lame jokes. I knew he suffered from depression, but I didn't know how that translated to so many afternoons in bed when I came home from school; I didn't understand what held him there beneath the sheets as I peeked through the cracked door to watch him sleep. I knew then it was pity I felt for him, but how to manage that pity I did not know, and so I only felt it as fear. In such moments I would have welcomed Dad walking naked down the hall looking for his razor. That would at least mean he was up and doing, proving to the world and his son that he was alive, that there was something worth getting out of bed for. After all, a parent is supposed to know a thing or two about waking up every morning to face the world.

I've often wondered about the virtue of that public-speaking admonition to imagine one's audience in their underwear. Such advice operates, I think, on the assumption that shame is a zero-sum game—that more squirm in the audience means less squirm in the speaker, as if the combination of insecurity and self-loathing we all occasionally feel could ever answer to anything so neat as an economic theory. As if self-doubt were a scarce resource. As if misery didn't love company. Shame may be the price we pay for being human, but we all pay it with our own unique currency, and we all end up wearing a barrel.

* * *

In an essay titled "Portrait of My Body," Phillip Lopate gives readers a tour of his physique, from the tilt of his frame, his slight shoulders, and the "intensity" of his head, to his "sad brown eyes" and his "long and not unshapely" legs. This is Lopate's literal tribute to the essayist as a navel-gazer, and we are privy to his bushy eyebrows, his several scars, and even the "ripe, underground smell" of, yes, his belly button. It's a self-deprecating undressing in which Lopate attempts to own his physical shortcomings, but it's also a celebration of sorts—the notes of a man sure in his own skin, eager to talk about the body as one might talk about a piece of antique machinery, a fine-crafted specimen made all the better for its wear.

But Lopate also spends nearly a third of the essay talking about his penis. To be sure, such crotch talk is rare, but not new in the canon of male essayists. Montaigne once dwelt for more than twenty thousand words on the "conjugal compatibility" of men and women and gave ample space to questioning the taboo of what he politely calls our "shameful parts." In the more recent past Edward Hoagland and John Updike have joined Lopate in exposing themselves for the sake of the essay. And anyone who has read David Shields would thank Hoagland, Updike, and Lopate for their discretion. But I think there's something problematic about such groin gazing, as if everything essential about male identity can be summed up in a close reading of one's crotch.

I do see something honest and thoughtful in the way Lopate publicly confronts his own self-consciousness—an approach that calls to mind the playful rebellion of a streaker at a football game. As a reader, I'm happy to laugh at his good-humored disregard for public decency and give a nod to a certain kind of bravado. But in the final third of the essay Lopate's candor begins to feel less like the liberating performance of a streaker and more like the sniggering self-satisfaction of a flasher. The first two-thirds of the essay says, "Look at me," while the last third says, "Look at this!"

A few years ago someone gave me a Shakespeare-themed magnetic poetry kit for my birthday, and it's been up on our fridge ever since. The set includes a bouquet of lovely Shakespeareisms: *forswear*, for instance, and *wonton*, and *saucy*, as well as some fantastic Elizabethan nouns that were new to my boys. *Bosom*, *wench*, and, among others, *codpiece*.

"What's a codpiece?" asked my oldest son, Callan, and ever since I explained, it's become a favorite ingredient in their impromptu poetry. Their latest musing to grace our fridge: "Methinks your wicked lady is a vulgar codpiece."

Such play is, methinks, the magnetic poetry version of the kind of play boys have been doing since boys learned the social significance of their own groins, the sort of play that leads to "sword" duels between brothers peeing into the same toilet, the same play at least partially to blame for Elvis Presley's pelvic thrusts and all those rappers grabbing their crotches, and maybe Lopate's essay (and maybe this one?)—the kind of play meant to settle fears that one's manhood might be little more than a joke.

And even though this play feels mostly harmless, I can't help but think of Margaret Atwood: men may be afraid that women will laugh at them, but women are afraid that men will kill them. There's an undeniably darker side to phallocentric preoccupations—virulent fixations on power that manifest in the bad behavior of grown men who've never grown up, men who carry such fear of emasculation that they treat every social interaction like some reptilian dominance ritual, men who let the hyperbole and misogyny of toxic male culture convince them it's okay to text out pictures of their genitalia, men who force themselves on coworkers or subordinates or strangers on crowded trains. Men like the one at a park in Spain who dropped his pants in front of my sister and her friends as they sat on the grass eating lunch, or like the nervous man I chatted with outside a church once who unexpectedly grabbed my crotch because, as he explained when I jumped back, he often worries about how he measures up, and he just had to check. Maybe there's no direct connection between codpiece jokes or rock 'n' roll pelvic thrusts and the awful behavior of predatory men, but I don't think it's unreasonable to acknowledge the common foundation of anxiety and self-consciousness that undergirds pretty much all performances of traditional male sexual aggression, however innocent or vile they may be. As the psychologists Woolfolk and Richardson put it, "The birthright of every American male is a chronic sense of personal inadequacy."

More than four hundred years ago, Montaigne recognized the problem: "Why . . . do we not value a man for what is properly his own? He has a great train, a beautiful palace, so much credit, so many thousand pounds a year: all these are about him, but not in him." The singular question that drove Montaigne's entire project was not "What do I own?" but rather "What do I know?"

And if Montaigne knew anything, it was that looking honestly at ourselves is both incredibly difficult and utterly necessary.

I always sort of knew that my father's incessant jokes and stories were rooted in a sense of inadequacy and a difficulty being himself in a crowded room, but I never much considered why he developed the habit of taking off his pants every time he came through the front door. Now though, I wonder if these two habits weren't related in some way—dropping trou as a subconscious counterbalance to his public clamors for acceptance. If his dominance of a conversation was an unspoken denial of his depression, then perhaps his shameless afternoons in his underwear were an unspoken acceptance of it.

Certainly Dad's depression revealed itself in other ways. His impotent rage when Mom grew impatient with him ("It's not like I'm having an affair," "It's not like I'm coming home drunk and beating the kids"), his dodging of phone calls from anyone he didn't want to speak with ("I'm not here," "I'll call them back," "Just let it ring"), his headaches that kept him from work and church and his kids' baseball games and extended family dinners ("I just took my medicine," "Give me a few more hours," "There's no way I could drive in my condition"). In those moments, all his hedging and hiding just seemed like odd cowardice to me, and I felt somehow we were complicit in his failures. If one of us just spoke up, if we said the right thing, maybe told him to put on some pants, then he'd have to change. As if cowardice was a fair word for any of it; as if change could ever be that simple.

* * *

Dad's twin brother, Richard, was the only member of the family who ever appreciated Dad's jokes, and recently Richard passed away. For the last ten years they'd met over lunch to exchange old stories, brag about their grandchildren, and compare notes on the little dogs they'd adopted to keep them company. Sure he and Richard passed around the same old jabs about which of them was better looking, but their conversations enjoyed the warmth of two friends long freed from the worry of trying to impress each other. I've heard them tell stories about growing up in the same abusive home, about taking their turns as runaways, about living on the street and sharing pocket change so they could both eat. These are not among the stories Dad tells freely, but when he and Richard got together the stories just came out. And it occurs to me that perhaps Richard was the only person with whom my father could ever be himself. And now that Richard's dead, I wonder, where does that leave Dad? For who knows better than a twin what it's really like live in someone else's skin? Who better than a twin to understand the truth that hides beneath our clothes?

Levinas argued that need is the natural state of humanity. All satisfaction, be it physiological or emotional, is fleeting. Need is the lowest common denominator. And shame, according to Levinas, arises when we cannot separate ourselves from this body that needs. Far from revealing our own insignificance, however, such shame, writes Levinas, reveals the "totality of our existence." In other words, discovering our own nakedness leads us to realize that everyone is naked and that we are all trying to escape ourselves. Such awareness is the beginning of empathy and the foundation of humanity.

I worry about my boys seeing me naked. Not literally, of course (I never walk naked down the hall before a shower), but emotionally. I know that just being a dad gives me a certain mythic quality that I haven't earned, but frankly, there are things I want to teach my boys before they stop believing in the mythology of me—things about getting out of bed every morning for work, about washing dishes on a Tuesday night, about showing up to baseball games, taking that garbage out, taking that phone call, that criticism. I worry that if they realize too soon just how human I am, they may stop listening. If Montaigne is right though, the most important thing they need to know is themselves, and if they never see me comfortable in my own weaknesses, how will they learn to be comfortable in their own? Sure I want them to know that for me, getting out of bed for work in the morning has never been a struggle, but they also need to know that sometimes getting out of bed to be a dad has been downright terrifying.

* * *

If that audience-in-their-underwear admonition applies to writing essays, then I guess I am supposed to imagine you, dear reader, in your underwear. So here it goes. You are sitting on the bus riding home from work, and you are now wishing you'd worn that new pair of Hanes, instead of the one that went through the wash with your favorite T-shirt and is now a delicate shade of purple. Or maybe you're sitting on your couch at home and, except for the fact that I've barged into the room, you're fine being there in your underwear. Statistically speaking, you've probably got a few more pounds on you than you'd like, hair in places you wish it weren't, and you may have a tattoo you regret or a birthmark most people don't know about or maybe a scar from a C-section or, like a friend of mine from high school, a long faint track running the length of your sternum where the doctors cut open your child chest to fix your heart. That scar stands out in my memory, not because I saw it often—only on the occasional trip to the pool—but because the scar was so long and evoked an image of my friend's ribs being pulled apart and the impossibility of such superlative exposure; his heart literally split open, his parents waiting somewhere beyond the closed doors of the operating room, and him on the table, sedated against the truth of his own body. Who among us could abide such an honest vision of ourselves?

The night we got word that Richard's condition was serious, I drove Dad to the hospital to say goodbye. I tried to imagine myself in Dad's position, going to visit his twin brother on his death bed, and wondered what he might say to him and also what it might be like for my uncle, surrounded as he was by red-eyed family who knew they could do nothing but smile, rub his feet, and wait for more bad news.

As we approached the hospital room, my aunt met us in the hallway. She looked tired and drained, and she held a tissue wadded up in her right hand. Dad began to say hello, but she cut him off. "No jokes," she said. "Not tonight. I just can't handle it."

When Dad moved to reassure her, she cut him off again. "I'm serious. No jokes."

My aunt had clearly been worried about Dad's visit, perhaps from the moment she knew we were coming. And it makes sense, caught as she was in the throes of unmitigated reality—her husband's body teeming with cancerous nodes and everything in her life about to change. I imagine anything less than the naked truth of the situation would have felt wrong to her. There could be no joking, no sugar coating—if she had to drop the façade, then so did everyone else.

And so we went into the room with bowed heads and soft voices. To Dad's credit, he behaved himself, nodding mournfully and asking polite questions about Richard's tests. He hugged his brother, and we all talked quietly, my aunt watching from the other side of the room. She had little to worry about though. Richard mostly wrote on a pad of paper because the cancer in his throat made talking difficult and banter all but impossible.

At some point, though, amid our long faces and gentle attempts to comfort him, Richard sat up and tried to mumble something to his brother. Dad, whose hearing has been bad for years, didn't catch what Richard said, so I put my ear closer to Richard's mouth. The reason I shouldn't have repeated my uncle is also the reason I couldn't resist: deathbed moments are for saying what really matters.

"Dad," I said, looking at my aunt briefly, not wanting to get in trouble. "Richard wants you to know that he's still better looking."

Despite my worries, I really do want to be seen for who I really am, both as a writer and as a parent, but both notions are scarier than I like to admit. Both require an uncommon level of vulnerability, a willingness to cut through the artifice, to own my history. Virginia Woolf wrote that sincerity is the cardinal virtue of the essayist; that's not an easy thing to offer a reader, or my boys. And it's not even a question of revealing dark secrets. The mundane truths are difficult enough: my insecurities about my body, my oedipal self-consciousness, the disconcerting possibility that my boys won't learn the lessons I'm still trying to teach myself. And then to put all that on paper or let my boys in on the facts? I find myself thinking, you want the truth? Sure, you can have the truth. Let me dress it up for you, tailor things to make a point. Use my father as a convenient way to package up my own sense of insecurity. Here's a bit of what happened, a taste of a moral, minus a bit of the awkwardness that doesn't fit the narrative. I'll explain when you're older. It's just a story. Do as I say, not as I do.

* * *

I admire the courteous confessions of the great essayists—Hazlitt and his love of hating, Woolf and her sense of impotence in an air raid, White and his affection for a dying pig. Their essays wander on a loose leash of propriety and proportion, determined to map the curious mind yet unwilling to dabble in what Woolf herself calls "unclothed egoism." These writers take their cues from Montaigne, of course, who understood that while "every man bares the full form of the human condition," choosing to essay the fullness of that form can be a "vain and frivolous" endeavor.

Consider Montaigne's twenty-thousand-word essay on conjugal compatibility. He gave it the enigmatic title, "On Some Verses of Virgil," and he meandered for three thousand words before coming to the real subject of that essay. Sure, we might chalk that up to sixteenth-century bashfulness, but I also think Montaigne's indirect approach makes a larger point—that the digressive nature of the essay reveals as much about the writer as any straight-forward confession. His opinions about the relative passions of married women and the dishonesty of decorative codpieces are as important to the essay's self-portrait as the frank frustration he expresses about the "pitiful vigor" of his own "shameful parts." Montaigne's insistence that he write himself "quite fully, and quite naked," was always about presenting a "more whole, and more life-like" version of himself—both the public and the private Montaigne: clothed and naked, vigorous and flaccid. Such confession becomes a problem only when done for the wrong reasons, when the essayist demands to be seen instead of helping others see themselves.

Recently I asked students to look for rhetorical situations in the real world where an essayist's perspective might do some good. One student looked at how self-deprecation and honesty could improve online dating profiles. Another considered self-reflection as a hallmark of artful punk lyrics. A third student made a compelling argument for emotionally raw, unfiltered honesty in social media posts. The most controversial presentation came from a student who asked, When a public figure finds him- or herself in the middle of a sex scandal or facing accusations of sexual misconduct, could the essay somehow help improve the public mea culpa that is sure to follow? His answer, after a systematic review of several high-profile statements from politicians, actors, comedians, and business leaders—no. The essay can do nothing in this situation. The problem? Motivation. The contrite public figure wants nothing more than the right words to make a story die. The essayist wants nothing less than right words to make a story live.

There's something I need to confess about my father's depression. It's been the source of a lot of pain and sadness in my family, but a selfish part of me has also been glad for it. I don't remember the first time I heard the Hemingway truism that an unhappy childhood is the best training for a young writer, but I know that in deciding how much to write about my father I've used those words as cover. And while my family's unique unhappiness has proven a Tolstoyish muse over the years, I know that the very claim of such unhappiness is, in its own way, unfair to my family and to my father, in particular. After all, when Dad blustered to my mother that he wasn't having an affair, that he didn't come home drunk or beat the kids, he was right. His bar for excellence may have been low, but he had a bar. The fact is, by Hemingway's metric, I feel more like E. B. White: "If an unhappy childhood is indispensable for a writer, I am ill-equipped: I missed out on all that and was neither deprived nor unloved." Still, to say my father did the best he could with what he had feels like a dishonest cliché designed to make us both feel better. In the end, though, what more can we ask from our children than a little graceful dishonesty?

The essay is a "naked, lonely, quixotic letter to the world," writes Scott Russell Sanders. But he also calls it "a one-man circus . . . which relies on the tricks of anecdote, memory, conjecture, and wit to hold our attention." To write an essay is never a matter of simply telling the truth. Certainly, we must get naked, but even in our most honest attempts to disrobe, we can't help but cover up.

* * *

As far as I can tell, Dad never got to say a proper goodbye to his brother. The day of Richard's funeral Dad was supposed to give the eulogy, and he'd planned to tell a funny story, one from their time together in the navy about Richard landing a job as a DJ for Armed Services Radio. Dad loves to tell how Richard, then an unranked seaman, shared airtime with Bob Hope, had his picture taken with Jayne Mansfield, and fulfilled song requests in exchange for rides around the base on the officers-only taxi service. It's the kind of story you want in a eulogy—sweet, laudatory, and short—and Dad even practiced with me the night before. He was so worried about rambling I offered to give him a signal from the audience if he got off subject.

The next morning though, I never got a chance to use that signal. I watched Dad stand up in front of the chapel full of people and watched him begin his story, but just a few moments in, he stopped abruptly, skipped over all the important details, and ended his remarks with a verbatim reading of the obituary printed in the program. He thanked the audience and descended from the podium but didn't sit down. Instead he disappeared out the door of the chapel and the service went on without him.

I'd find out later that in the middle of Dad's story, my aunt had cut him off, had actually given him a show-biz-style hand across the throat from her place in the front row. I understand now how she must have been feeling, wrestling with her own grief, worried about the audience and the danger of a funeral dragging on, and I know she must have been concerned about Dad's tendency toward long-winded asides, so I can sympathize with what she did. But in that moment all I understood was that Dad had been at the pulpit standing above Richard's casket, looking for words to give his brother a meaningful send-off, and the microphone was all but pulled from his hand, leaving him alone in front of all those people, wearing nothing but the stark face of a bewildered man with no story left to conceal him.

Brenda Miller once wrote, "The body knows a language the mind never wholly masters," and if that's true, then perhaps nakedness is the most difficult of dialects, with a syntax and grammar we stumble upon only through experience. Few things in this world exert as much control over us as the naked body. Whether attracted or repulsed, we are ultimately arrested, even for the briefest of moments. The question of course, for all of us, is not whether we hear the language of the body, but rather how we choose to respond.

In the last scene of his essay "Once More to the Lake," E. B. White describes himself sitting in a rented cabin in the aftermath of a summer storm. "Languidly, and with no thought of going in," White watches his son put on a wet bathing suit. White is an old man now, long since done with the cold-lake plunges of a storm-dark afternoon. Instead, he watches his son "wince slightly as he pulled up around his vitals the small, soggy, icy garment," and in a vortex of nostalgia and memory White feels "the chill of death." He is both his son and his father, simultaneously young and old, alive and dead. And though this moment skirts the edge of sentimentality, that too feels like an important part of White's confession—a nod to nostalgia's role in bridging the gap between boyhood and manhood, an acknowledgment that a father's body is not his own, that a son's body is not his own, and that the truth of our collective nakedness might just be the most important truth we ever learn.

Montaigne wondered if our fear of death had more to do with the "dreadful faces and trappings" of ceremony than with any fact of death itself: "The cries of mothers, wives, and children . . . people dazed and benumbed by grief . . . a darkened room, lighted candles . . . in short, everything horror and fright around us." With death, as with nakedness, it takes some getting used to, and we hurt ourselves only by living in denial. "We must strip the mask from things as well as from persons," writes Montaigne. To be alive is to be naked and unprepared for death. To live is to acknowledge these facts, first in ourselves and then in others, and in these facts find courage to forgive ourselves for being human.

That day at Uncle Richard's funeral I sat the entire service in a row beside my boys—Callan right next to me, then Nolan beside him, and Ian at the end. They each wore their best slacks and white button-down shirts, and I could tell that morning they'd all tried extra hard to comb down their hair. We shared a hymnbook, and they sang all the songs, and I only had to remind them once or twice to sit up straight. Dad's flubbed eulogy aside, the service was sweet in all the ways a funeral should be, but my mind kept coming back to that image of Dad staring at his twin brother in a casket—that rarest of moments when a man can stare death and himself in the face at the same time. All this got me thinking of my own brothers sitting a few rows back, of my boys sitting in the row beside me, all of us lined up as if waiting our turn; it was at this point that I began crying the requisite and inevitable tears of a funeral. Beside me, Callan shifted in his seat, and then I felt a thin arm light on my shoulder, a rare gesture of empathy from this often-aloof teenager, and he leaned his head against my arm and let me cry. Then a few moments later he turned to me and said, "I saw in the gym where lunch is set up. They've got chocolate cake."

Worry Lines

I.

I look concerned. Nolan, our middle child, tells me as much one night while we sit reading together on the couch.

"Where did you get those lines?" he asks and runs a finger across my forehead. I lift my eyebrows and allow him to press his finger into the furrows of my skin. I shift my brow up and down and pull a goofy face until he giggles.

"Those are my worry lines," I tell him, and we drop into a conversation on the topography of faces, on crow's-feet and frown lines and the forces of gravity, age, and sun damage that will eventually change his boyish complexion into a tired, creased one like his father's. "You'll have them someday too," I say. "But not for a long time."

What I don't say is that gravity, age, and sun damage are really only part of the story. I don't explain that we call them worry lines for a reason; that anxiety, stress, exhaustion, and fear can engrave themselves on our faces. That for some these lines might mean "marriage is impossible," or they might mean "I don't know how I'm going to feed my family," or "what if my cancer comes back," or "how am I supposed to raise this boy in such an ugly world?"

What I don't say is the thing he'll eventually figure out on his own: that whether we like it or not, all of us wear our faces like a metaphor.

2.

"Worried," is not the adjective George Zimmerman used on the evening of February 26, 2012, when he called 911 to report a "real suspicious guy" walking through the neighborhood. But worry is the word. "This guy looks like he's up to no good," he told dispatchers from his car. "Or he's on drugs or something."

There'd been a rash of break-ins around the neighborhood. Doors had been forced open. A laptop stolen, a bicycle too. Strange young men lurking on lawns, peeking in windows. One woman hid with her son in a bedroom while invaders tried to steal her television.

In the year prior to Trayvon Martin's death, residents had made more than four hundred calls to police.

Zimmerman was studying criminal justice. He worked as a fraud investigator for a local insurance firm, and he captained his neighborhood watch. Several times in the past year, he'd called police to report suspicious behavior, and the suspects, according to Zimmerman, were always Black.

"Assholes always get away," said Zimmerman to the dispatcher, shortly before hanging up and getting out of his car. Zimmerman didn't like bad guys, and the police were slow.

The "bad guy," in this instance, was Trayvon Martin. You know his story. A seventeen-year-old boy visiting the neighborhood with his father. He'd made this visit several times, and that night he'd walked to 7-Eleven for a snack: Skittles and a can of juice. Zimmerman's "real suspicious guy" was on his way home from a convenience store. His hoodie was up. The rain had begun to fall.

3.

On Wednesday evenings in the predominately white suburb where I live, my boys attend youth night at a church down the street from our house. They play basketball and soccer, plan campouts, and eat junk.

Occasionally, when they're bored, they talk their youth leaders into playing a game they call 007. The boys fan out into the neighborhood on foot, and after a good head start, the leaders follow in a car. The rules are simple. Get from one side of the neighborhood to the other without the adults catching you. Good, clean fun.

It's not uncommon to see boys hiding in the bushes, cutting across lawns, crouching behind parked cars, and hiding under hoodies while bemused youth leaders roll slowly down the street, eyes peeled.

4.

Trayvon Martin noticed George Zimmerman at about the same time Zimmerman noticed him.

A car slows down in the rain. A strange man follows a teenage boy with his eyes. The boy stops and looks back at the man in the car. Trayvon is worried. He's on the phone with a friend, and he tells the friend he's being watched. That he's being followed.

"Run," says the friend. "You better run!"

When Trayvon Martin takes off, Zimmerman gets out of his car. "He's running," Zimmerman tells the dispatcher, and he curses. Over the phone comes the sound of wind and hard breathing. The dispatcher wants to know if Zimmerman is following the boy. "Yeah," says Zimmerman.

"We don't need you to do that," says the dispatcher, and his voice sounds worried.

A few moments later, Zimmerman hangs up. He's still agitated by the "suspicious" young Black man in the hoodie walking around the neighborhood. He sets off after him, and a few moments later, Trayvon Martin is dead.

5.

Every year or so we buy new hoodies for our boys, or at least a new one for our oldest son, Callan. The ones he grows out of get passed down the line. Callan prefers his hoodies black, and he wears one almost every day, the drawstrings pulled even, the hood left down to avoid messing his hair. Nolan likes a zipper, but the color doesn't matter. When he's sitting outside, he draws his knees to his chest and pulls the hoodie over his legs to stay warm. Ian, our youngest, wears hand-me-down hoodies that always start out a little too big. The sleeves hang unevenly on his shoulders, and the unzipped sides flap in the wind as he runs.

I'm raising three white boys in the suburbs, and when one of them wears a hoodie, it's always just a hoodie—a practical bit of outerwear, comfortable and convenient. We worry about them getting cold. They worry about wearing a bulky jacket at school. The hoodie is a win for everyone.

6.

According to the people closest to him, Trayvon Martin was a good kid. His father, Tracy Martin, and his mother, Sybrina Fulton, describe Trayvon in their memoir, *Rest in Power*. "My son had been a life force, a teenager who had hopes and dreams and so much love," writes Tracy Martin.

Trayvon played junior league football, worked at his father's business, and got decent grades. He planned to study aviation, he listened to music nonstop, and he worked odd jobs to pay for his growing collection of Air Jordans.

Sybrina Fulton described her son as "a mama's boy, always with me, always affectionate."

As he got older, "his teachers generally found him pleasant and smart. But there were some dark clouds, too," writes his mother.

His junior year Trayvon started skipping classes, his grades slipped, he vandalized a locker—he ended up with a ten-day suspension from school. "He was a good kid," writes his mother. "But Tracy and I started to worry."

Later, after Trayvon's story became headline news, conservative talking heads would point out that Trayvon's Twitter profile showed a picture of him flipping off the camera; they would remind their audience that Trayvon had a tattoo, that he smoked weed, that he must have dealt drugs, that he was six foot two, and that he dressed like a "thug."

On Fox News, Geraldo Rivera said, "I think the hoodie is as much responsible for Trayvon Martin's death as George Zimmerman was."

7.

As a parent, I've got a lot I can worry about. What are the boys doing on the computer? What are they texting their friends? What music are they listening to? Who are they hanging out with at school? Are they talking back to their teachers? What's really in those sci-fi novels they can't put down, that video game, that TV show with all the angsty teenage kissing?

I worry in general that all three of my boys will be meathead teenagers who drive too fast and never say "thank you."

I worry they'll let their meathead friends talk them into teenage hijinks like egging houses and snowboarding off the roof.

Someday, I tell them, you'll find yourself on a Friday night hanging out with other boys, and you'll need to be the voice of reason—I show them grainy YouTube videos as evidence: a boy squealing in pain when a lit firecracker explodes in his mouth, a boy slamming into a mailbox as he's towed on a sled from behind a pickup truck, a boy breaking his elbow as he tries to pull a handstand on a skateboard. Endless videos that all offer the same lesson—being careless can get you hurt.

8.

Tracy Martin recalls some of the advice he received when he was a young man: "The first thing that was instilled in me was to be patient, careful, and respectful to everyone I met, not just because it was the right thing to do, but because it could be the difference between life and death."

He tells of some white boys in a passing car who threw bottles and shouted the N-word at him and of how that car turned around and how he remembered his mother's counsel. "If you see somebody coming at you with any kind of racism, run."

Tracy Martin continues, "I told my kids, including Trayvon: 'If you see yourself about to get into a racial confrontation, eliminate yourself from the equation.'"

Writer Liz Dwyer describes the fear—"poisonous at its core"—that she felt after the birth of her son: "I was now responsible for raising a Black child and, in America, that means my kid is always in danger."

Laura Murphy, former director of the ACLU Washington legislative office, writes about what she calls the "disturbingly contradictory signals" she and other Black parents send their children about how to be safe in a white world. Walk too quickly and you'll look suspicious. Walk too slowly and you'll also look suspicious. Don't hang out with too many friends because you'll look like a gang, but don't wander by yourself because you'll look like you're up to something. And yet, Murphy writes, "there is essentially nothing that parents can tell their Black children—especially young men—about how to survive in this world that will protect them from violence."

Cartoonist Barbara Brandon-Croft describes worrying about her own son in a similar way. "I had to give the Trayvon talk to my son and his friend as they headed out to the park last night. . . . I told [them] that if they are approached by anyone of 'authority' (fake cops included) that they had to be ultra polite ('Yes, sirs' and 'Yes, ma'ams'). . . . I told them that although it may not be fair, I would rather have them humbled than harmed . . . or worse."

9.

Speaking on the day of George Zimmerman's not-guilty verdict, Barack Obama said, "If I had a son, he'd look like Trayvon Martin." Today, I think, *I have three sons, and none of them look like Trayvon Martin*. But that's not entirely true.

Callan is about the same height and weight, same build. Has the same love for music, same preoccupation with girls, same affinity for hoodies.

I describe Callan as "pleasant" and "smart," the way Trayvon Martin's mother has described him, and I've seen those "dark clouds" that can hang over a teenager's days.

How, then, do I explain my knee-jerk inclination to see these two boys as different? Prejudice? White privilege? A lack of imagination? Something else?

"Empathy is tricky," writes journalist Sherronda J. Brown. "We can only identify with the pain of others through the understanding and profound feeling of our own suffering, but that only exists when we are able to recognize a shared vulnerability."

In essence, I'm predisposed to see Trayvon Martin as different from my son, not merely because Trayvon Martin is Black, but because in this country, his Blackness and my whiteness mean that there are real limits to our shared vulnerabilities.

To call these boys different risks perpetuating the notion that racial violence is not my problem. But to call these boys similar risks downplaying the consequences of racial violence altogether.

10.

"How can I show you the hole in my heart?" writes Sybrina Fulton in the introduction to *Rest in Power*. "It's almost impossible to convey the devastation and pain, the bottomless loss, heartbreak, and helplessness—the feeling of being broken into pieces that will never come back together again."

I want to say I understand. That I have some idea of what it would be like to lose my son the way Sybrina Fulton and Tracy Martin lost theirs. But even writing that sentence feels like an overstep.

As if "lost" were a sufficient word for what happened to Trayvon. As if my white son could ever be taken from me the way Trayvon was taken from his parents. As if I could ever fathom the true weight of American racism.

Perhaps the most radical empathy I can embrace as a white person, then, is to admit that given the full cultural, historical, and psychological context of what it means to be Black in America, it may be a genuine impossibility for me, and for most white people, to ever understand what Trayvon Martin's family has gone through.

11.

What's missing from the story of Trayvon Martin is Trayvon Martin's side of things.

We have only his parents' memoir, a friend's testimony, and the recording of a bystander's 911 call that has preserved a boy's voice yelling for help; also, the few photographs online: the bright smile of several snapshots and the haunting gaze of that hooded selfie.

But there is that other witness—the killer and what he saw, the stereotype he indulged, and the image he perpetuated—the Black teenager in the hoodie, "suspicious," "up-to-no-good," "on drugs or something."

Not to mention the brawling pundits, the internet conspiracy theorists, the dueling politicians. Trayvon was a saint or he was a thug; either he never saw it coming or should have known he had it coming.

As if the whole country saw Du Bois's "double consciousness" play out in Trayvon Martin's story on cable news: "This sense of always looking at one's self through the eyes of others, of measuring one's soul by the tape of a world that looks on in amused contempt and pity."

12.

"Because white men can't police their imaginations, black men are dying," writes Claudia Rankine.

Because my white sons will grow up to be white men in America, they must learn to police their imaginations, and I must teach them how.

But is it enough to hold a little family tribute to Martin Luther King Jr. every January? Or enough to watch Neil deGrasse Tyson on *Cosmos: A Spacetime Odyssey*, or enough to play the *Hamilton* soundtrack on Saturday mornings while we clean the kitchen?

Of course not.

They still get up each morning and go to a school where they're surrounded by so many other white faces, and how can their world feel anything but right to them—white and right.

We need to have a Trayvon Talk of our own.

"We can't actually teach humans to have no prejudice at all," writes Robin DiAngelo. Instead, what we often do is teach our children to pretend prejudice does not exist. "Ideally, we would teach [our children] how to recognize and challenge prejudice, rather than deny it."

Which may be one reason I am writing this essay.

And one reason I worry so much about writing this essay—my little nod to white privilege before I retreat to my typical oeuvre: teenage romance, parenting guilt, and my somewhat dysfunctional childhood.

Du Bois writes, "All art is propaganda," but I wonder, propaganda for what?

If this essay is my halting attempt to recognize and challenge prejudice, how often does the rest of my life effectively deny that prejudice exists at all?

13.

If YouTube can offer my boys a primer course on teenage stupidity, then what can it teach them about prejudice, privilege, and the dangers of the white imagination?

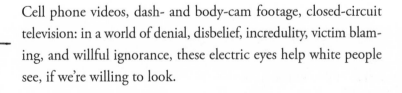

Cell phone videos, dash- and body-cam footage, closed-circuit television: in a world of denial, disbelief, incredulity, victim blaming, and willful ignorance, these electric eyes help white people see, if we're willing to look.

Videos of white people calling the cops on Black kids for selling water without a permit, on Black men for barbecuing in the park or waiting in a Starbucks, on a Black student for falling asleep in the common area of her own dorm, on a Black couple for checking out of their Airbnb, on a Black babysitter for eating with two white children at a Subway.

Not to mention videos of more deadly white violence—cops gunning down kids playing in the park or shooting Black men during routine traffic stops.

Routine—that's the word, and that's a problem.

But from all this, what lesson? Consider James Baldwin: "It is the Black condition, and only that, which informs us concerning white people."

14.

In *Between the World and Me*, Ta-Nehisi Coates explains to his son that it took becoming a parent to understand the tight grip of his mother's hand, and the fear and love she felt for him. "She knew that the galaxy itself could kill me, that all of me could be shattered and all of her legacy spilled upon the curb like bum wine. And no one would be brought to account for this destruction because my death would not be the fault of any human but the fault of some unfortunate but immutable fact of 'race,' imposed upon an innocent country by the inscrutable judgment of invisible gods."

Tracy Martin writes, "I knew the justice system wasn't color-blind. There's one set of rules for us and a different set for other groups. . . . The rules for us—for African Americans—had been in place for a long time in this country. And the rules were not going to help us. So from the beginning, I was worried."

According to Sybrina Fulton, the prosecutor's opening statement came down to a simple question: "Who was more afraid in the moments before the confrontation, the seventeen-year-old minding his own business? Or the grown man with a loaded gun?"

With no definitive witnesses and no way to get Trayvon's side of the story, Zimmerman's lawyer would successfully argue self-defense. "No injuries are necessary to respond with deadly force," said the lawyer in his closing arguments. "The statute is clear—a reasonable fear of bodily harm." Zimmerman had the right to stand his ground.

In other words, Trayvon Martin is dead, but his death is no one's fault. The law is the law. Our hands are tied.

Or worse, Trayvon Martin has no one to blame but himself. If he hadn't been walking through that complex in the rain. If he hadn't been wearing that hoodie. If only he'd kept running. If only he hadn't asked the man with the gun, "What are you following me for?" If only he hadn't stood his ground.

15.

"His is the story of a life cut tragically short," writes Trayvon Martin's mother. "But it's also the story of a boy who in death became a symbol, a beacon, and a mirror in which a whole nation came to see its reflection."

And it's Sybrina Fulton's last metaphor that has me thinking. If Trayvon Martin is a mirror, does he, like a mirror, reflect only what stands before him? Does what I see in Trayvon Martin depend more on what I bring to the encounter than any fact of his life?

Perhaps Trayvon Martin's death is an embodiment of Black tragedy, or a consequence of white delusion; certainly his death and the uproar that followed underscores the great and terrible racial divide in America, but before all that, he was a son and a brother and a friend, a human being built of love and mystery and infinite possibility.

How can we ever build a bridge to span America's racial divide if we do not build it from this reality—what should be the first facts of every human life? What progress can be made if white America does not embrace the humility and compassion necessary to get to know boys like Trayvon Martin well before they're transformed into metaphor?

16.

When my son Nolan asked me about my worry lines, he did not realize he was asking one of the oldest questions of the American experience—namely, what's there to learn by merely looking at a person's face?

He has no idea how often our history has turned on that question. How often we've failed as a nation by getting that question wrong.

I love that he's paying attention though, that he's looking around with such careful eyes, brimming with curiosity, and laying the groundwork for a few worry lines of his own.

In a world where too many people are convinced they have all the answers, I find some hope in a twelve-year-old with a heart full of questions.

Apocalypse, Now?

The first concept that got into [our] heads
was the idea of life and death,
that the sun went down and the sun went up.
That the crops died.
In the winter, everything died.
The first man, he must have thought,
"Oh my God, it's the end of the world!"

—FRANCIS FORD COPPOLA

Things fall apart; the centre cannot hold;
Mere anarchy is loosed upon the world.

—WILLIAM BUTLER YEATS

The voice of the wild evangelist echoed down the street. "DAM-
NATION!" It bounced off the buildings all around us. "REPENT!
JESUS WILL SAVE YOU!" My oldest son, Callan, looked to me
and said, "What's that?" But before I could answer, we'd turned
the corner, and there he stood a few yards in front of us: a tall man
in knee-worn denim with long hair that might best be described
as "the Jesus look." In this memory, I draw my family close to
me as we scurry to the far side of the block like extras in some
disaster film. But in reality, we merely kept our distance and

tried to ignore the man as he held forth on that curb in front of a Quiznos in Boise, Idaho.

Nearby, a father eating with his children at an outdoor table paused midbite to stare, as if in the middle of a sunny summer day, fiery hail had started falling from the sky. He stood up and approached the man. "We're trying to eat our dinner," he said, and his voice sounded conciliatory, reasoning. The preacher turned to meet him, but instead of apologizing, he pointed a finger at the father. "You," he said with a spit. "You probably think I'm one of those extremists." The father stepped back, and the preacher turned again to the street. "THE END OF THE WORLD WILL COME!" he shouted. The father stood for a moment, as if struck dumb, and then gave up. "THE END OF THE WORLD WILL COME," I heard the preacher say again. "ARE YOU READY TO DIE?"

The father gathered his family and moved on, and so did we, and soon enough we were out of earshot and on to the rest of our pedestrian day. However, the preacher's question stayed with me. "Am I ready to die?" If he'd confronted me, my answer would have been simple. No, I'm not.

I suffer from what Charles Lamb called an "intolerable disinclination to dying." Not that I'm afraid of death, per se, but of leaving everything behind. "I am in love with this green earth," writes Lamb. "The face of town and country; the unspeakable rural solitudes, and the sweet security of streets." To Lamb's list I might add the gleam of skyscrapers on sunny city mornings; the satisfying leather pop of a baseball mitt at the park; an evening of my children snort-laughing at the dinner table; the salivating enthusiasm of my dog at ten in the evening as she places a wet tennis ball at my bedside, eager for the field across the street.

When I enumerate the million small beauties of the earth, I want to say I cannot fathom the apocalyptic motivation of that haggard preacher on the street. I want to say the world is such an impossibly wondrous place that praying for its destruction seems to me like the height of insanity. But a cursory glance at the week's headlines is enough to make just about anyone wish for a giant reset button on humanity: "New Chemical Weapons Attack in Syria"; "Parents Accused of Torturing Their 13 Children"; "86 Men Arrested in Sex-Trafficking Bust"; "Another Child Dies in ICE Custody." It's the prophecy of Yeats come true on the nightly news—the best seem to "lack all conviction," while "the worst are full of passionate intensity."

And that's just the headlines. Every neighborhood in the world plays host to a thousand minor cruelties every day: parents coerce their children; siblings belittle one another; neighbors gossip, covet, and ignore the people living right next to them. The other day my sister accidentally cut off an oversized pickup at an intersection, and the driver followed her into a parking lot and jumped out, looking for a fight. My sister is five foot four, and if she hadn't been with her husband and my older brother, who knows what would have happened. Everyone got out of their cars and stared at each other across the pavement, and a too-long moment passed before the driver got back in his truck and drove away. I talked with my brother right after the altercation, and he was still breathing hard. "I guess when it comes down to it, we're all just a bunch of chimpanzees," he said. But if that were true—if we were all just animals—the cruelties we commit might not feel so cruel. Survival of the fittest makes sense when we're talking about a sick calf cut from a herd of wildebeests by hungry lions or an unsuspecting mouse lifted from some neighborhood field by a swooping hawk, but the great paradox and promise of humanity is that we expect each other to be humane. At our best, our capacity for compassion is the greatest miracle of the natural world, but at our worst, there's not much about humanity worth saving.

* * *

For two years right after high school I served as a missionary for the Church of Jesus Christ of Latter-day Saints and did my own share of street preaching, but I was less beast-slouching-toward-Bethlehem and more nineteen-year-old-boy-stumbling-through-Hiroshima. I never used a megaphone or sandwich board, never commanded anyone to repent, and I never warned anyone of the apocalypse. Mostly I taught people in pain. Like the seventy-year-old woman who'd spent the last decade running a river-dredging company because her husband had died unexpectedly and left her the business. And the Nu Skin distributor who wore the same blue suit every day and occasionally slept on the street; the salesman who'd suffered such trauma when his father died that whole chunks of his memory had disappeared; the twenty-two-year-old who'd been visiting his comatose father in the hospital every day for years; and the mother who lost her toddler in a fireworks accident and just wanted to know that he was okay, wherever he might be.

One effect of spending twelve hours a day talking with strangers about God was a heightened sense of how many of us there really are on the planet and—though the observation may seem patently obvious—how human we all are. I remember landing in Osaka on my first night in Japan and taking the train through that sprawling metropolis—a million lives zipping past me out the window—and I remember thinking how surreal everything looked. This entire city of shopkeepers, bicycle commuters, truck drivers, and children walking with their parents, all with their own preoccupations and passions, and all that bustle repeated a hundred million times every day across the country. The immensity of humankind means it's easier to imagine everyone else as backdrops to our own story rather than the truth—that there is just one story, and it has no backdrop.

* * *

In the first battle scene of Francis Ford Coppola's 1979 Vietnam film, *Apocalypse Now*, Captain Willard and his crew land their patrol boat on the beach at the edge of a bombed-out Vietcong village. The scene is a pandemonium of smoke, falling artillery, and flailing palm trees. An amphibious troop carrier rolls up out of the water and demolishes a bamboo hut. Soldiers throw grenades, and a colonel named Kilgore strolls through the chaos in his cowboy hat, counting dead bodies and bragging about his surfboard and how he likes to "finish operations early" and "fly down to Yung Tau for the evening glass." As he chats about surfing, mortars continue to fall, and flames light up the background. Fearful villagers cram into transports, helicopters roar up above, and a television crew records it all. Meanwhile a priest in a flak jacket performs Mass for a congregation of disheveled troops, and, as the camera pans out to take in all the mayhem, we hear the soldiers repeat the Lord's Prayer. In the background, a solitary helicopter rises in the sky, a water buffalo in a cargo net dangling beneath it, silhouetted against a smoky sunrise.

This scene makes a telling microcosm of the modern world. Right now mortars are all but certainly exploding in some corner of the world. Somewhere a priest conducts Mass for a gathering of war-ravaged congregants, and somewhere else a group of desperate men are begging for their lives. Women and children somewhere are crouched low while bullets fly overhead, and somewhere a warmongering colonel shoots the breeze with a gang of sycophants. In the background of it all cable news teams record everything for first-world consumption.

At times the entire planet seems to be on fire, but it's almost always somewhere "over there," which means that from the relative comfort of my living room I have options. Depending on my political leanings, I can tune in to CNN or MSNBC or Fox and sigh in disbelief at all the misery I see; I can pick up a phone and donate to Doctors Without Borders or Planned Parenthood or the NRA; I can get on Twitter and tell the world how blessed I am to live in the United States or maybe add my two cents' worth of liberal guilt about white privilege and the patriarchy. If I'm feeling particularly moved, I might attend a protest, or a counterprotest; I could even visit a sick neighbor or volunteer at the food bank or my local elementary school. What's more likely? A little mini apocalypse of my own—I'll decide that the world and all its anger and suffering is just too exhausting, and with a simple press of the button, I'll make it all disappear.

* * *

After serving in Japan for a year, I'd begun to feel pretty comfortable. I remember one afternoon seeing a white person across the street and saying to my companion, "Hey, look, it's a *gaijin*," which is to say "foreigner" or literally "outsider." I'd come to think of myself as an "us," not a "them," and most of the time that's how I imagined Japanese people had come to see me.

Once though, I bumped into a man with my bicycle and got a quick lesson on in-group/out-group sociology. The man owned a T-shirt shop near our apartment, and though we never spoke to him, we often waved, and he usually waved back. One evening though, as we were heading out, I saw the man closing his shop and decided to stop and talk with him. As my companion rode on, I pulled up to the man on my bicycle and asked him for a moment of his time. He waved me off and said something about heading home, so I swung back up on my bicycle and turned around, intending to offer him a good night and catch up to my companion. However, I misjudged the angles and hit the back of the man's foot with my front tire, causing him to trip and nearly fall.

I can see the whole scene from his perspective—a pushy American missionary bothering him on the way home from work, vindictive about the abrupt rejection, looking for payback. I don't remember the exact words he yelled at me, but I remember his white-hot anger. I asked what I could do to make things right, and he told me I could leave Hiroshima, that I could leave Japan and never come back. I stood there holding my helmet, and who knows how long he would have yelled at me if my companion hadn't returned to finally smooth things over. More than a year I'd spent trying to convince people in Japan that we were there to help if they wanted it, and I had never considered that I might be a nuisance. My companion promised that we'd come back the next day with one of our local leaders to formally apologize, and the man finally let us go. We got on our bicycles, and I followed my companion off into the night, a red moon shining over us, the stars falling from the sky.

* * *

A recurring joke at our house when the news gets ugly: "Can we just vote for Jesus?" The notion being that if Jesus were in charge, then everything would be okay. Except that all depends on which Jesus we're talking about. My Jesus would be really into social justice. He'd be all about immigrant rights, and he'd want to close the gender pay gap and enroll everybody in a good healthcare plan, and he'd grumble in general about the inhumanity of unfettered capitalism. He'd open up more soup kitchens and remind the NRA about that whole "swords into ploughshares" scripture, and he'd roll his eyes at a baker unwilling to decorate a cake for a gay wedding. But what if a different Jesus showed up? A gun-toting, prosperity-gospel Jesus, a survival of the worthiest Jesus who prioritizes bootstrap capitalism and Western birthright over everything else. I don't want that Jesus in charge of anything.

And what if the Jesus who showed up proved even worse than that—the Jesus of that street preacher in Boise, ready to burn us all? Years ago I met an evangelist in Ohio who carried a megaphone and wore a sandwich board that read in large letters: REPENT NOW OR BE DAMNED, and beneath that was a list of sinners, which included the usual suspects: liars, fornicators, murderers, and perverts; but his "going to hell" list also included Democrats, environmentalists, "new agers," loud-mouth women, Mormons, and even Catholics. With that Jesus in charge, there wouldn't be many of us left to save.

Of course, the Bible offers plenty of evidence for a socially conscious Jesus who turns the other cheek, feeds the hungry, and declares, "He that is without sin among you, let him first cast a stone." But those hellfire street preachers aren't making up their sermons out of nothing. Sure I might roll my eyes at what I see as misguided fundamentalist zeal, but as a Christian I've got to face the uncomfortable reality that hellfire street preachers are, like it or not, part of my tribe. And that's not even the real issue. Even if you're ambivalent about the garden of Eden, even if you're more comfortable with the notion of Noah's ark or Balaam's ass as metaphors rather than historical realities, if you believe Jesus was more than just some grand philosopher, then you've got to come to terms with the Jesus who preached of pestilence and famine, of earthquakes in divers places, of wars and rumors of wars, that Jesus who warned of false prophets and violence and the hearts of men turned cold; you've got to acknowledge the fact that Jesus himself was, in some ways, a wild man in the street preaching the end of the world.

For many Christians this apocalyptic Jesus is all too easy to embrace. In Texas, I remember seeing a bumper sticker that read, "In case of rapture, this car will be empty." I thought the sticker was a joke at first, but then from another preacher outside the mall I got a pamphlet outlining the details of this Rapture—a miraculous event just before the end of the world when all the righteous will be lifted up into the clouds so the remaining detritus of humanity can be burned to a crisp. What this means, essentially, is that many Christians, who are commanded to be merciful, to make peace, to go the second mile, are also watching with giddy anticipation for Jesus to come again and get them the hell out of here. Humanity's problems are too overwhelming, says apocalyptic thinking; the earth is a rusty, sputtering jalopy, and eventually God will decide he's dumped all the money he can into keeping it on the road. Someday soon he'll tell all his children to get out, and he'll drive the old clunker into a ditch, light the whole thing on fire, and buy a new one for the long drive into eternity. Perhaps another reason I resist embracing the Apocalypse is that holding out for the end of the world simultaneously feels like giving up on everything else.

* * *

A decade after coming home from Japan, I stood in my brother's living room in Salt Lake City and watched as CNN aired footage of a massive tsunami striking the northeast coast of Honshu. A magnitude 8.9 megaquake originated forty-five miles off the coast of the Tohoku region, and shook for six minutes, creating a tsunami several meters tall that traveled toward the mainland at roughly five hundred miles per hour. Residents had less than ten minutes of warning, and the tsunami came with such force that whole neighborhoods were lifted off their foundations and dragged along with the water like so much driftwood; cars piled up like toys and churned down city streets, and debris caught fire atop the water, creating blazes that burned the entire first night. In the end, more than fifteen thousand people died, and more than three hundred thousand lost their homes. The quake actually shifted the earth on its axis, and the tsunami caused a nuclear meltdown at a power plant in nearby Fukushima.

When I lived in Japan, I heard stories of the great Hanshin quake of 1995 that killed six thousand people in Kobe, but that quake had a magnitude of 6.9 and had lasted only twenty seconds. By the time I passed through Kobe six years later, everything had been rebuilt. Staring in disbelief at images of the Tohoku tsunami in 2011, I could hardly imagine anyone could rebuild after such a disaster. But in Japan earthquakes are a given and so is resilience. They build skyscraper foundations deep into the ground and support them with shock-absorbing springs and dampers; they've constructed a billion-dollar network of sensors that report seismic activity from all over the country and miles of concrete seawalls that protect nearly all the inhabited coastline. Schools hold regular earthquake drills, and many families have earthquake survival kits at the ready.

Devastating earthquakes are relatively rare in Japan, and major tsunamis rarer still, but when one does come through, life eventually goes on the same way it does in Florida between hurricanes or Kansas between tornadoes or California between wildfires. So many of us going about our business in the face of so much potential devastation. And that is the image that has stayed with me as I've reviewed footage of the disaster: so many panoramic views of the Japan I lived in, with its narrow streets and busy grandmothers and rumbling trucks going down the road and just on the horizon, but moving quickly, an apocalypse.

* * *

Yeats envisioned the end of the world approaching as a giant, lumbering sphinx.

Somewhere in sands of the desert
A shape with lion body and the head of a man,
A gaze blank and pitiless as the sun,
Is moving its slow thighs, while all about it
Reel shadows of the indignant desert birds.

In Egypt the sphinx guarded tombs and honored dead rulers, but the Grecian sphinx—the riddling executioner—is what I picture in Yeats's apocalyptic vision. After all, what is the Apocalypse but a grand, perplexing puzzle with endless possible explanations, any one of them just us unlikely as the next? And there may be something the beast of Yeats's poem can teach us about apocalypse that the ancient myths do not. That is, in real life you don't have to be on the road to Thebes to find yourself in trouble; rather, in matters of the end of the world, the sphinx will eventually come to you.

* * *

A few months after the Tohoku tsunami, a branch of my church in the region began housing volunteers who could spare a few days to help the cleanup efforts. My wife and I had donated a bit of money back when the disaster was still fresh in everyone's mind, but the offering hadn't felt like much. I told my extended family that I planned on raising money to go, and my brother, my cousin, and her daughter all decided to make the trip with me. We arranged ten days for travel, put out the word on social media, asked friends and relatives for donations, and gathered enough money to pay for our tickets to Tokyo.

We arrived in late July and took a bus to Miyagi Prefecture, where we met Hiroyuki and Chiyoko Asano—the service coordinators who would be directing our work. We spent several days on their volunteer crew working in Ishinomaki City, in a devastated neighborhood near the coast. Many of the houses were gone, and many that survived sat crooked on their foundations. Down one street an eighty-foot boat sat in the middle of a field. Down another street we saw a white minivan still wedged on its side between two houses. Empty shells of apartment complexes stood guard over what, from some angles, looked like a ghost town. And yet we saw progress everywhere. Nearly all of the destroyed homes had been scraped away, and tons of loose rubble had been piled up in massive trash heaps around the city. The neighborhood felt more like a construction zone than a disaster zone. A few homes had even been restored, and we saw plenty of signs of domestic life—the radio playing through an open window, laundry billowing on back porch lines, and pots of bright flowers set out on the occasional porch.

We spent most of our time cleaning out just one building—a ten-unit row of townhomes. The water had risen as high as first-story ceilings, which meant the ground floors were a complete loss. Furniture and appliances were lifted and tossed by the flood, while dishes, books, and magazines spilled out and settled into several inches of mud that covered everything. We hauled away fridges full of rancid food, made a pile at the curb of water-logged electronics, bagged up sludge for special disposal, and shoveled endless piles of unrecognizable debris.

The work offered a satisfying sense of purpose, but I also remember feeling a little selfish. As pure as our intentions were, our trip amounted to little more than some voluntourism, and I couldn't help but wonder whether the Red Cross or some other charity could have put our money to better use. Still, we had done *something* in Ishinomaki. By the end of our stay our crew had cleaned out all ten townhomes in that building and helped make the place ready for rehab work. And there was another consequence that I hadn't expected. Walking each day through the aftermath of such wild destruction awoke in me strange emotions I've felt at few other times in my life: a sorrow that calls to mind the day my best friend's five-year-old boy passed away; a surge of adrenaline that reminds me of a predawn drive years ago when I ran a stop sign and just missed the front end of a large truck; a dull fear straight out of one of my recurring nightmares about my car going off the road into a river, my children trapped in the backseat. The whole experience became a reminder of what I can't bear to lose, a primer in tragedy, especially the unexpected kind; the trip was ultimately an invitation to accept that for all of us, the end may be closer than we can imagine.

* * *

In *The End of the World: An Annotated Bibliography* anthropologist Tom McIver catalogs texts from Western culture's obsession with apocalypse from prehistory to the most recent millennium. His bibliography contains more than 3,400 entries, the first of which references the Book of Enoch, an ancient Jewish text supposedly written by Noah's great-grandfather. Enoch writes of fallen angels who corrupt humanity by mating with human women and of God's impending judgment on the wicked. The last bibliographic entry references Thor W. Zollinger, a Lockheed-Martin engineer who, in the late 1990s, published online a fifteen-chapter, eighty-six-thousand-word, scripture-based prognostication about the end of the world. Using the first Iraq War as his reference point and relying on various Old and New Testament timelines, Zollinger predicted The End could come as early as 2013. Sandwiched between the Book of Enoch and this Book of Zollinger we find a colorful panoply of scriptural exegeses, theological musings, and prophetic warnings from writers famous and obscure. Of his bibliography McIver writes, "What the works in this collection have in common is that all are convinced the world is coming to an end . . . and that this End constitutes a divine judgment." Put simply, this book shows us that for as long as we've been thinking about our own existence, we've contemplated the question of who deserves to live and who deserves to die, and the answer has almost always been "we do, and they don't."

McIver's book also shows that apocalyptic thinking is old. Perhaps as old as consciousness itself. A fundamental part of human awareness is, after all, the knowledge that one day each of us will die, that individual annihilation is not merely a possibility but an outright certainty. And if we only had Mother Nature's earthquakes, floods, fires, and plagues to worry about, apocalypse might not be such a central theme in human history. But all that pales compared to what we have done to each other. Some scholars trace apocalyptic thinking back to that moment in deep history when two competing tribes first migrated into the same fertile valley. By this point we'd long established that what we hunted and gathered today might not be around tomorrow. Animals die or migrate; berries wither on the vine, rot in the basket, or disappear into the bellies of our greedy cousins. But it wasn't until one tribe sharpened their spears and raided the camp of another that our awareness of scarcity gave way to the notion of injustice and the terror of impotence. If everything we possessed could be wiped away in a blink and we were powerless to stop it, then our only hope was divine intervention—an apocalypse.

* * *

On the morning of the earthquake, the Asano family had been helping at a friend's flower shop. When the quake began, they escaped outside to the parking lot and held each other through that long, relentless shaking. Then they got in their car and headed toward their home on the coast, but a tsunami warning came over the radio, and they were met on the road by a stream of cars fleeing to higher ground. At the same time, they felt a change in the atmosphere that Chiyoko described as "an uncomfortable, heavy tingle, compressed, and dreadful." They turned their car around and drove inland with the other traffic, and five minutes later the first tsunami waves hit, destroying much of the nearby coastline, including their neighborhood.

They slept those first two nights in their car, eating snacks from a convenience store and relying on the caretakers of a Buddhist temple who shared their toilet and offered them a little food. On day three the Asanos checked in to an evacuation site at an elementary school several miles inland from their destroyed home. There they spent close to three weeks sleeping first in the gymnasium and then in the library, rationing food and supplies that arrived intermittently, and trying to make the most of their time with other evacuees. They followed along with a morning calisthenics broadcast on the radio, took turns cooking and cleaning, helped new evacuees settle in, and played games with the children, even holding a small birthday party for a girl who'd just turned six.

Despite their hopeful response to the disaster, the Asanos had no home, no work, and no idea what the future held. But then phone service was restored, and a friend from a congregation in nearby Furukawa called with an opportunity. He explained that donations of food and supplies had been pouring in to their little branch from all over the country, and he wanted to know whether the Asanos could help manage it all. They took the job, and by May they were living in their own apartment in Furukawa, and their days were full delivering care packages to affected neighborhoods and organizing cleanup crews. When we met them they welcomed us like old friends and put us to work like family. They shuttled us from site to site, coordinated with other volunteer groups, and even fed us a goodbye dinner on the night we left.

For all their energy and good nature, the Asanos struggled for months after the disaster to make sense of everything. "We tried to keep a record in a notebook we found, but we could hardly write because . . . our minds and hearts could not keep up with the reality," writes Chiyoko. It would be July before they could look at a budding flower and appreciate its beauty. "Seasons transgressed in silence. Even though cherry blossoms bloomed . . . and trees turned green, we felt nothing." What ultimately helped? Not rebuilding their own lives but helping rebuild the lives of others. "We had the chance to do volunteer work there, which healed our hearts," writes Chiyoko. In the tsunami, the Asano family lost nearly everything, but in its aftermath they discovered for themselves a small miracle. Chiyoko writes: "We hope to continue helping brighten up the lives of as many people as we can."

* * *

When Coppola decided to take a film crew into the Philippine jungle in the late 1970s, he was riding high from the successes of the *Godfather* movies. He had the freedom to work on any project he chose, but he gambled on *Apocalypse Now*, a retelling of Joseph Conrad's *Heart of Darkness* set during the Vietnam War. He wanted to uncover some truth about America's involvement in the war, but he also wanted to uncover something true about himself as well; as his wife, Eleanor Coppola, put it, he wanted to "confront his fears—fear of failure, fear of death, fear of going insane."

Whatever Coppola hoped to get from the project, what his audiences got was a psychedelic war film that painted American interventionism as mad folly. In *Heart of Darkness*, Captain Marlow takes a steamboat up the Congo River to bring relief supplies to a rogue ivory trader named Kurtz who has set himself up as a god among the natives. In *Apocalypse Now*, Captain Willard takes a navy patrol boat up the Nung River on a secret mission to assassinate a rogue colonel Kurtz, who has likewise set himself up as a god among the natives. In Conrad's novella, Kurtz represents the arrogance of European imperialism and the folly of assuming that "Western" culture should be the model for the rest of the world. In *Apocalypse Now*, Kurtz represents the problem of American imperialism and the folly of assuming that American democracy should be enforced by military might. Both versions of Kurtz show us the pitfalls of the assumption that Western "progress" is a universal good.

As a film scholar friend of mine explains it, *Apocalypse Now* was important because it looked back on the Vietnam War and said, "We weren't the good guys over there." The movie underscored the absurdity of war and reveled in those absurdities: trigger-happy cavalrymen, calculating commanders, doped-up soldiers trained to kill anything that ran from them—chaos and confusion and boredom and trauma, all for dubious political and moral reasons. As Coppola explained, "My film is not about Vietnam. It is Vietnam . . . We were in the jungle. There were too many of us. We had access to too much money, too much equipment, and little by little, we went insane." For many audience members, the movie helped reveal some unsavory realities about the American military industrial complex, and it also helped destroy the very American notion that whenever we felt like it we could sharpen our spears and raid the village next door. In this dual way, the title of the movie makes perfect sense, for *apocalypse* comes from a Greek word that means "revelation," but over the centuries, has, of course, evolved to mean "total and complete destruction."

* * *

Less than three days after the Tohoku disaster American conservative media personality Glen Beck described the earthquake as a possible "message from God" about obeying the Ten Commandments. "I'm not saying God is causing earthquakes, but I'm not not saying that either." Only a day after the tsunami, Tokyo's governor told reporters that the devastation was "God's punishment" for Japan's "egoism." A famous Russian movie director said that Japan's "inner godlessness" caused the disaster, and an outspoken Muslim sheikh pinned it all on Japan's unwillingness to accept monotheism. The consensus was simple: God had been looking down on Japan from his cloud, and he was really mad, and they got what was coming to them.

Anyone who pays attention to the news coverage after a major natural disaster will recognize such empty moralizing. Pundits and preachers made similar claims after Hurricane Katrina in 2005 and the Sumatra tsunami in 2004. More recently a Colorado radio preacher blamed California's wildfires on the state's acceptance of homosexual lifestyles. One of the more appalling accusations came back in 2009 from televangelist Pat Roberts who blamed the earthquake in Haiti and its two hundred thousand casualties on nineteenth-century Haitian rebels who "made a pact with the devil" to secure their freedom from France.

It might be Noah's fault that as a culture, we're often so quick to give an angry God credit for the awful things that happen. And if God is in control of the lightning and the wind and the great seismic plates that heave ocean waters beyond their bounds, then I guess he could roll out Mother Nature as a tool for exercising judgment, but then how to account for all the sunny days of calm that fill the broad gaps between the violence? If a tsunami is punishment for something, then are the birdsong days of spring a reward? And for what?

* * *

Among the great mysteries in Christianity, three stand out—the Creation, the suffering of Christ on the cross, and the Apocalypse. These mysteries are great because they address the most fundamental questions about existence—where we came from, why we're here, and where we're going. And they're mysteries because, well—the answers are mysterious. Look at any major world religion, and you'll find mysteries that address these same fundamental questions. Ancient teachers and texts are often explicit about rites, rituals, and commandments, but when the subject turns to one of these mysteries, all resort to imagery, symbolism, allegory, and myth. Because the answers to such questions are unknowable, we experience them in metaphor; in Christianity, creation is the Spirit of God brooding upon the waters, a division of light and dark, a calling forth from the dust, the plucking and shaping of a rib. The sacrificial Christ is a pure lamb, a bridegroom, the bread of life, and a fountain of living water. In the Revelation of John, readers experience the end of the world as sounding trumpets, a seven-headed dragon, a series of horned beasts, the mother of harlots "drunken with the blood of the saints," and the earth turned to a sea of glass. Set these apocalyptic images of John beside the clear-cut commandments of Christ's Sermon on the Mount and one wonders—what is the point of such deep symbolism? Perhaps the answer has to do with art itself—for what is the language of these great mysteries but the language of poetry—our best attempts to express the inexpressible. The purpose of commandments is to dictate a certain way of life, but the purpose of art is to inspire new ways of living.

All the more reason then to bemoan the way John's apocalyptic poetry gets reduced to a catalog of tortures the Almighty just can't wait to unleash upon the earth. When I was in high school a quiet man in a leather jacket used to stand just off school grounds and pass out pamphlets to students on their way home. The pamphlet

I remember most contained a poorly drawn comic depiction of the fiery judgment that awaited me if I failed to repent. Flames licked the edges of each illustration as guilt-ridden teenagers writhed in agony. While I attended Brigham Young University in Provo, Utah, a similar man often loitered near campus and passed out pamphlets on why I, as a member of the Church of Jesus Christ of Latter-day Saints, was in particular danger of hellfire. And in my own religious community, though we may not embrace aggressive street preaching or comic depictions of hellfire, we can be just as quick to self-righteous judgment as anyone.

Why does such prejudice come so easily for most of us, regardless of our feelings about religion? When I think about that Ohio street preacher with the megaphone, what stands out to me is not the length of his list of the damned but of how comfortable he seemed assigning complete strangers to such an awful fate. At its most elemental level, it seems apocalyptic thinking demands a confirmed posture of us-versus-them, of persecuted and persecutor. Someone saved and someone damned.

The very history of Western eschatology is, in fact, a history of the human family wishing violence on one another. In 1982 Yuri Rubinksy and Ian Wiseman published a survey of apocalyptic thinking titled *A History of the End of the World*. The book charts a correlation between historical moments of violence and a yearning for The End. The Jews of the Old Testament, for instance, endured the slaughter and captivity of Babylon, trusting a Messiah would eventually come to redeem them from their enemies. Early Christians watched for the fall of Rome as a signal that Christ would finally restore himself, and his people, to power; early Crusaders believed that by freeing the Holy Land from Muslim "heathens," they could complete the restoration that their ancestors never achieved; survivors of the Plague in Europe saw all that death as a cleansing preparation for Christ's Second Coming. Many

European explorers were driven, at least in part, by a desire to overthrow the "evils" of paganism by spreading Christianity "to the ends of the earth"—a biblical requirement for triggering the end of the world. British imperialism, American Manifest Destiny, and even the Nazi fever dream of a thousand-year Reich were all, in part, fueled by millennial zeal—a mythology of salvation through bloodshed underwritten by the promise of liberation, restoration, and prosperity.

Consider the paranoia of the Y2K nondisaster, the knee-jerk military response to the September 11 attacks, the conspiracy theories about Barack Obama being the anti-Christ. Today apocalyptic thinking is as prevalent as ever. In 2010 Pew Research found that 41 percent of Americans believed the Second Coming of Christ was at least "probably" going to happen before the year 2050. In 2012 at the height of the Arab Spring, half of Muslims surveyed believed that Yawmuddin—the Muslim version of Judgment Day—waited just around the corner. And in the wake of that social uprising, the terrorist group calling themselves ISIS capitalized on residual apocalyptic anticipation by leveraging ancient Islamic prophecies, end-times rhetoric, and doomsday imagery to recruit followers, legitimize violent land grabs, and justify the indiscriminate murder of thousands.

Apocalyptic thinking has always been about "chosen" people and "chosen" land—who owns it, who stole it, and whose blood needs to be spilled in order to protect it or reclaim it. ISIS, for instance, intended to slaughter their way across the globe until, as their propaganda put it, "their blessed flag . . . covers all eastern and western extents of the Earth, filling the world with the truth and justice of Islam and putting an end to the falsehood and tyranny" of infidels and their democracy. That sounds crazy, but it also sounds familiar, at least if you've been paying attention to white supremacist rhetoric here in the United States—mostly delusional white men pining for a future where North America becomes a white ethno-state purified of racial diversity through a disturbingly euphemistic process called "peaceful ethnic cleansing." And as with ISIS, so to with white supremacists; you can hear the apocalyptic preoccupation with land and displacement in their chants as they marched in the streets of Charleston, Virginia, in 2017. In their khaki shorts and white polos, they held aloft their hardware-store tiki torches, screaming about blood and soil and chanting "You Will Not Replace Us," their strained voices echoing the battle cry of every apocalyptic movement of the past three thousand years.

* * *

Near the end of our second or third day working in Ishinomaki, the Asanos drove us to a nearby elementary school. "I want to show you something special," said Hiroyuki. We parked just outside a large school building, and he led us through a pair of double doors into a gymnasium lined with rows of tables and hanging racks full of family photos, portraits, diaries, genealogical records, and other personal documents.

In the weeks following the tsunami, rescue crews went house to house looking for survivors and recovering bodies, and along the way they began salvaging important family documents as well. Boxes of recovered items were collected first at police stations and then in shelters. Expert conservators cleaned, separated, and protected each item, and all restored items were brought to makeshift conservatories, such as this elementary school, where they would rest until survivors came looking.

We spent about twenty minutes viewing the photographs and other items laid out so neatly before us. Snapshots of parents squeezing their children, stern-faced couples in formal wedding attire, smiling students in their matching uniform. The scene reminded me of the photo collages I've seen at funerals—a parade of images that span a lifetime. But walking through that gymnasium, we were not meant to mourn the dead. Instead, the whole space felt like a waiting room for memories, all that evidence of life reclaimed from the mud, cleaned, preserved, and holding out for survivors. The entire room a testament to the best of humanity in the face of tragedy; proof that more important than the questions of what was destroyed or why, are the questions of what can be salvaged, and for whom.

* * *

In the final act of *Apocalypse Now* Willard and what's left of his small crew arrive upriver at the ancient temple where Colonel Kurtz has established the headquarters of his makeshift jungle kingdom. Willard is met on the shore by a strung-out photojournalist with a cultish respect for Kurtz: "You don't talk to the colonel . . . you listen to him," he says. "The man has enlarged my mind." As the pair makes their way up the steps of the temple, Kurtz's native acolytes follow, wary of Willard as a potential threat to their king. Dead bodies spill over rock ledges and severed heads lie on the jungle floor. Bodies hang from trees. And there in the background, on the wall of the temple, we see the title of the film graffitied in white spray paint: "Apocalypse Now." No one ever says the phrase in the movie, and you might miss it in this scene if you're not looking for it. It's a subtle move in a film that rarely banks on subtlety and suggests an important point—that the end of the world does not await us in a dark, distant future, but rather it looms everywhere in the immediate present. And while I find the argument of *Apocalypse Now* depressing, I think there's something to the suggestion that we are in the middle of an apocalypse of sorts—that we are always at the crossroads of our own making, a choice between revelation and destruction, of knowledge and annihilation.

* * *

Of all the messages I shared with people on the streets of Japan— short lessons on prayer or faith or forgiveness—the message that resonated most often was charity: "Though I speak with the tongues of men and of angels, and have not charity, I am become as sounding brass, or a tinkling cymbal. And though I have the gift of prophecy, and understand all mysteries, and all knowledge; and though I have all faith, so that I could remove mountains, and have not charity, I am nothing." What made these verses so popular? The simple mathematics of it: combine eloquence and prophecy and mysteries and knowledge and faith, and what you get still can't measure up to pure love. After all, what is the value of the fiery sermon or the heavenly vision or the apocalyptic terror of a mountain displaced when set alongside the miracle of one human sacrificing for another? If apocalyptic thinking is born in persecution and violence, what Paul seems to be arguing for as the highest form of godliness is a willingness to set aside such affronts. If "charity suffereth long" and "is not easily provoked," then charity must be, by definition, more interested in the pres- ervation of mankind than in its destruction.

Brian Doyle once wrote, "No God can forgive what we do to each other; only the injured can summon that extraordinary grace." His point? For whatever forgiveness that may or may not await us in the great beyond, the forgiveness that we need so desperately here can come only from those we've offended. Likewise, whatever great and terrible End awaits the world from supernatural powers, the End we probably ought to concern ourselves with most is the one we risk inflicting upon each other.

* * *

According to Rubinsky and Wiseman, believing in a great End to the world helps us give "reason and purpose to all that has gone before." By embracing an apocalypse, we attempt "to make sense of life," and we discover "where life is most vulnerable and in what ways most fragile." As Rubinsky and Wiseman write, "Every End teaches mortality." The problem, though, is that every End doesn't necessarily teach morality: "Mankind's fascination with the end, in all its picayune detail, accomplishes the remarkable: it saves us from the difficulty—in fact, the impossibility—of having to imagine life without an end." In some ways by embracing apocalyptic thinking of any kind, we give ourselves a way out—an excuse to care less about the people in that collapsed building on the other side of the world, less about refugees afloat on the oceans, less about that old woman living across the street. But, say Rubinsky and Wiseman, "What if life were infinite? What if the fragile earth was to be our home forever? How would we face that possibility?"

For one answer, consider the famous riddle of that sphinx in Yeats's poem. What animal first walks on four legs, then two, and finally three? The solution that eluded everyone but Oedipus, the answer the sphinx was waiting for, the key to keeping her destruction at bay—was us. You and me. Human beings. *We* are the revelation that defuses our own potential destruction. Humanity is the mystery—but also the answer to everything.

* * *

I recently logged in to Google Maps and went hunting for that neighborhood in Ishinomaki where my brother and I worked with the Asano family. What had become of the townhomes we'd worked on, I wondered. What of the surrounding houses and shops, the piles of garbage that rose on the horizon like small mountains? I typed in the address, and the map took me right down to street view where the panoramic image showed the neighborhood more or less as we'd left it—the shell of a warehouse waiting for new life, the piles of trash waiting for collection, the row of townhomes sitting scoured and empty. But when I zoomed out for a bird's-eye view of the neighborhood, the image was more recent, and everything had changed. The warehouse had been razed, along with our row of townhomes and several other houses on the block. All the debris had been cleared away, and a few new homes had sprung up out of the dirt. I zoomed out farther on the map so I could take in the whole neighborhood, then the whole city. Gone were the fishing boats listing in rice fields, the giant mounds of trash; no more wrecked cars stacked like Legos, no more houses teetering on foundations. Just a still image taken a few months ago of a city well on its way to recovery.

The miracle of my computer offers a view of the world that previous generations might have thought reserved for the gods, and the click-of-a-button mobility never ceases to amaze. One second I'm looking down on my own backyard in Utah with its dry-patch grass and overgrown trees, the next I'm panning across three thousand miles of ocean and zooming in on a medium-sized city in northern Japan. Click and drag that screen in any direction and eventually I'll come to a town or village or city that, from above, looks a lot like so many other cities in the world, give or take a few sunny days or years of trouble. Ishinomaki could be Istanbul could be Indianapolis—a calico patchwork of rooftops and treetops, stitched together by an endless maze of roads flanked by shopkeepers busy in storefronts, hurried commuters walking down sidewalks, and a constant caravan of trucks and cars emerging from the horizon. If Google could zoom in far enough to see through those rooftops, it could, given sufficient time, collect enough evidence to call down fire and brimstone on every last one of us. But, given sufficient time, it could also collect enough evidence to keep any apocalypse on hold indefinitely.

Artists like Francis Ford Coppola want to remind us about the terrible things we are capable of doing to each other, and we don't have to look very hard to see the evidence. In Yeats's poem I see something similar—a wariness of the world and an urge to warn us of impending doom. And our news and entertainment and religion often thrive on the same impulses. But looking down from the heavens on the crowd of houses in my neighborhood, or the ones in Ishinomaki, or in any corner of the world, I find myself less interested in the fiery fate that may or may not await any of us and more interested in the endless ways so many of us have found, in spite of so much destruction, to go on living.

A NOTE ON NOTES

In my own private writing fantasy, I imagine that I'm working in the armchair tradition of essay all-stars like Montaigne, Emerson, Woolf, and Baldwin; that my work feels at home in the William H. Gass definition of the genre: "Born of books, nourished by books, a book for its body, another for its head, and hair, its syllable-filled spirit, the essay is more often than not a confluence of such little blocks and strips of text." And what follows is a bibliography of sorts that I hope at least acknowledges my attempt to, as Montaigne put it, "make others say for me . . . what, either for want of language or want of sense, I cannot myself so well express." But in the age of information, I find my essays are less born of books than they are born of Google. Sure, in the source material for this collection you'll find books, articles, personal interviews, and the shadow of at least one Freedom of Information Act request, but the thrill of the archival hunt has largely been replaced by the convenience of the digital deep dive. In the words of Nicholas Carr, "Research that once required days in the stacks or periodical rooms of libraries can now be done in minutes. A few Google searches, some quick clicks on hyperlinks, and I've got the telltale fact or pithy quote I was after."

This wouldn't be a problem except that according to Phillip Lopate, "The pleasure of knowing that we are in cultivated hands, attending to a well-stocked, liberally-educated mind, is a central attraction of the personal essay." And it is hard to claim those cultivated hands or a well-stocked mind when I rely so completely and hopelessly on the internet. At times it seems all I've really gained in my twenty-first-century liberal education is a deft mastery of the keyword search. Again, Nicholas Carr: "What the Net seems to be doing is chipping away my capacity for concentration and contemplation. My mind now expects to take in information the way the Net distributes it: in a swiftly moving stream of particles. Once I was a scuba diver in the sea of words. Now I zip along the surface like a guy on a Jet Ski."

Perhaps essays then are one answer to the frenetic tendencies of the internet. In "Essay as Hack," Ander Monson writes, "The essay . . . processes ideas, images, texts, or objects at its own speed. It rewinds, meditates, circles, returns, sits and spins if it must. And it should. It is, like all good art, an interruption, an intervention between the world and the mind." If all of us need to increase "our capacity for concentration and contemplation" and slow down the "swiftly moving stream" of the internet, then perhaps the essay is just the literary tool the world has been waiting for. Certainly I could not have written these essays without the help of the internet, but perhaps what you and I will need to survive the age of information is a little help from the essay.

NOTES

Delusions of Grandeur

In the age of Google, drumming up sage commentary on delusion in human nature requires little more than the right set of keywords. Still, finding such widespread concern about delusion from such a broad spectrum of prophets, theologians, philosophers, musicians, and poets felt, if not revelatory, then at least serendipitous. And the fact that all these luminaries stress the danger of delusion suggests two things—first that overcoming our delusions is a major step toward salvation, enlightenment, true happiness (or whatever you want to call it). Second, that most of us have a long way to go.

The biblical references here come from Ecclesiastes 1:14 and 2 Timothy 3:2. The other references are as follows:

Angelou, Maya. "A Brave and Startling Truth." In *Celebrations: Rituals of Peace and Prayer*. New York: Random House, 2011.

Baldwin, James. "The Discovery of What It Means to Be an American." In *Collected Essays*, 142. New York: Library of America, 1998.

Du Bois, W. E. B. "Science and Empire." In *Dusk of Dawn*, edited by W. E. B. Du Bois. Piscataway NJ: Transaction, 1984.

Itivuttaka 11. "Itivuttak: The Buddha's Sayings." Sutta Central. https://suttacentral.net/iti11/en/ireland.

Johnson, Samuel. "No. 28. The Various Arts of Self-Delusion." *The Rambler*, no. 28 (June 23, 1750). www.johnsonessays.com.

Lennon, John, and Paul McCartney. "Strawberry Fields Forever." *Sgt. Pepper's Lonely Hearts Club Band*. EMI Records, 1967.

Montaigne, Michel de. "Of Practice." In *Complete Essays of Montaigne*, translated by Donald Frame. Palo Alto CA: Stanford University Press, 2002.

———. "Of the Affection of Fathers to Their Children." In *Essays of Montaigne*, translated by Charles Cotton, edited by William Carew Hazlitt. London, 1877. Project Gutenberg, 2006. www.gutenberg.org.

———. "Of the Education of Children." In *Essays of Montaigne*, translated by Charles Cotton, edited by William Carew Hazlitt. London, 1877. Project Gutenberg, 2006. www.gutenberg.org.

Quran. Al-Hadid 57:20. www.quran.com.

Solnit, Rebecca. Introduction to *The Best American Essays 2019*, xvii. Edited by Rebecca Solnit. Boston: Mariner, 2019.

Wollstonecraft, Mary. *A Vindication of the Rights of Woman*. London, 1792. Project Gutenberg, 2002. www.gutenberg.org.

Woolf, Virginia. "The Decay of Essay-Writing." In *Selected Essays*, edited by David Bradshaw, 5. Oxford: Oxford University Press, 2009.

Toy Soldiers

Years ago as a student, I read Scott Russell Sanders's first essay collection, *The Paradise of Bombs*, but I only recently picked it up again and was surprised to read him describe the gun lust of his 1950s boyhood in much the same terms that I have described my boyhood thirty years later. In particular, his description of the comic book soldiers hit a particularly familiar chord, though in my mind G. I. Joe is the animated series, not the comic book: "In the gaudy cartoons the soldiers had seemed like two-legged chunks of pure glory, muttering speeches between bursts on their machine guns, clenching the pins of grenades between their dazzling teeth. Their weapons had seemed like tackle worthy of gods." In addition, I was pleased to read the description of his own toddler turning his bread into a weapon: "One day at lunch, still frustrated in his desire for an honest-to-goodness gun, Jesse nibbled his peanut butter sandwich into the shape of a revolver and sprayed us all with bullets." Subconscious though it may have been, I seem to have channeled Sanders in this piece, and for his excellent example of a father essaying his way toward clarity, I am grateful.

I should also call particular attention to Kenneth D. Brown's 1990 article, "Modelling for War? Toy Soldiers in Late Victorian and Edwardian England," originally published in the *Journal of Social History* 24, no. 2, which provided so much excellent historical context and a gold mine of a bibliographic information. Other sources include:

Archer, John, ed. *Male Violence*. London: Routledge, 1994.

Brown, Kenneth D. "Modelling for War? Toy Soldiers in Late Victorian and Edwardian Britain." *Journal of Social History* 24, no. 2 (1990): 237–54.

Edmunds, C. *A Subaltern's War*. London: Peter Davies, 1929.

Gergen, Mary M., and Sara N. Davis, eds. *Toward a New Psychology of Gender*. London: Routledge, 1997.

Kimmel, Michael S., ed. *The Politics of Manhood: Profeminist Men Respond to the Mythopoetic Men's Movement (And the Mythopoetic Leaders Answer)*. Philadelphia: Temple University Press, 1995.

Larsen, Knud S. *Aggression: Myths and Models*. Chicago: Nelson-Hall, 1976.

O'Neil, James M. *Men's Gender Role Conflict*. Washington DC: American Psychological Association, 2015.

Prinz, Jesse J. *Beyond Human Nature: How Culture and Experience Shape Our Lives*. London: Allen Lane, 2012.

Sci-News Staff. "Archaeologists Find Viking Age Toy Boat in Norway." Sci-News, March 7, 2017. www.sci-news.com.

Shaver, Phillip R., and Mario Mikulincer, eds. *Human Aggression and Violence*. Washington DC: American Psychological Association, 2011.

van Vugt, Mark, David De Cremer, and Dirk P. Janssen. "Gender Differences in Cooperation and Competition: The Male-Warrior Hypothesis." *Psychological Science* 18, no. 1 (January 2007): 19–23.

Wells, H. G. *Little Wars: A Game for Boys from Twelve Years of Age to One Hundred and Fifty and for That More Intelligent Sort of Girls Who like Boys' Games and Books*. London: Frank Palmer, 1913.

Good Enough

This essay is the product of a rabbit-hole research expedition that began with curiosity about prescriptive grammar and arrived at the good bishop Robert Lowth and his intrepid biographer, Ingrid Tieken-Boon van Ostade. Her phenomenal research on both Lowth and the history of prescriptive grammar provided an excellent analog for questions about moral prescriptivism and the true nature of goodness. Anyone interested in the history of English grammar should give TBVO's scholarship a gander.

I should also note that in quoting from Tobias Wolff's short story "Bullet in the Brain," the em dash that replaces the F-word was all my doing. Call me delicate, but this book is going to sit on my shelf at home, and I've got three boys who aren't allowed to use the F-word, so I figure my book isn't either. Apologies to Mr. Wolff.

Beal, Joan C. *English in Modern Times*. London: Arnold, 2004.

Brown, James. *An Appeal from the British System of English Grammar, to Common Sense*. Philadelphia: John Fennemore, 1836.

Burke, Seán. *The Death and Return of the Author: Criticism and*

Subjectivity in Barthes, Foucault and Derrida. 2nd ed. Edinburgh: Edinburgh University Press, 1998.

Cheshire, Jenny, and Dieter Stein, eds. *Taming the Vernacular from Dialect to Written Standard Language*. London: Longman, 1997.

Collins, John. *Chomsky: A Guide for the Perplexed*. London: Continuum, 2008.

Crowley, Tony. *Standard English and the Politics of Language*. 2nd ed. London: Palgrave Macmillan, 2003.

Crystal, David. *Making Sense*. London: Profile Books, 2017.

Dossena, Marina, and Charles Jones, eds. *Insights into Late Modern English*. Vol. 7. Pieterlen and Bern: Peter Lang, 2003.

Emerson, Ralph Waldo. "Divinity School Address." July 15, 1838. www.emersoncentral.com.

Freeborn, Dennis. *From Old English to Standard English*. 2nd ed. Ontario: University of Ottawa Press, 1998.

Gottman, John M., and Nan Silver. *The Seven Principles for Making Marriage Work: A Practical Guide from the Country's Foremost Relationship Expert*. New York: Three Rivers, 1999.

Heron, Robert [John Pinkerton]. *Letters of Literature*. London: G. G. J. and J. Robinson, 1785.

Leitner, Gerhard, ed. *English Traditional Grammars: An International Perspective*. Amsterdam: John Benjamins, 1991.

Lowth, Robert. *A Short Introduction to English Grammar: With Critical Notes*. London: J. Dodsley, 1774.

Milroy, James, and Lesley Milroy. *Authority in Language*. 4th ed. New York: Routledge, 2012.

Mouffe, Chantal, ed. *Deconstruction and Pragmatism: Simon Critchley, Jacques Derrida, Ernesto Laclau and Richard Rorty*. New York: Routledge, 1996.

Pinker, Steven. *The Sense of Style*. New York: Viking, 2014.

Poldauf, Ivan. *On the History of Some Problems of English Grammar before 1800*. Czech Republic: Nakladem Filosoficke Faculty, University Karlovy, 1948.

Reynolds, Jack, and Jonathan Roffe, eds. *Understanding Derrida*. London: Continuum, 2004.

Robinson, Ian. *The New Grammarians' Funeral*. Cambridge: Cambridge University Press, 1975.

van Kemenade, Ans, and Bettelou Los, eds. *The Handbook of the History of English*. Oxford: Blackwell, 2006.

van Ostade, Ingrid Tieken-Boon. *The Bishop's Grammar*. Oxford: Oxford University Press, 2011.

———, ed. *Grammars, Grammarians and Grammar-Writing in Eighteenth-Century England*. Berlin: Mouton de Gruyter, 2008.

Watts, Richard J. *Language Myths and the History of English*. Oxford: Oxford University Press, 2011.

Whitman, Walt. *Leaves of Grass*. London, 1886. whitmanarchive.org

Williams, Joseph M., and Joseph Bizup, eds. *Style: Lessons in Clarity and Grace*. Fort Worth TX: Pearson Education, 2014.

Stuck

The earliest version of this essay was a two-page lyric description of my first visit to the plasma center. And while almost nothing from that initial draft has remained in the final version published here, such preliminary attempts to capture the emotion of an experience have often proved a necessary first step in my work. In that early draft I recorded one of my favorite memories from donating plasma, and it killed me to cut it from later drafts. However, when the creative nonfiction gods bestow upon you certain conversations, you've got to find a way to share them. So here it is:

Jason, my phlebotomist, told me about his side business breeding scorpions, tarantulas, and reptiles. How he started about six months ago. How business was going well before he had a "serious setback," which was a euphemism for leaving an enclosure open for six baby ball pythons to escape, and how he'd only recovered two of them, and how the idea of four baby snakes crawling around their property did not sit well with his wife. He told her he was just going to get rid of everything, but he'd only said that in the heat of the moment, "mostly out of anger." And he told me how he was planning to "pull back a little until things cool down, and then I'll get back into it." And he pulled out the needle to stick me, and he said, "I've got snakes that weigh more than I do."

Buckley, Geoffrey L. *Extracting Appalachia: Images of the Consolidation Coal Company, 1910–1945*. Athens: Ohio University Press, 2004.

Crowell, Douglas L. *History of Coal Mining in Ohio*. Columbus OH: Dept. of Natural Resources, Division of Geological Survey, 1997.

Darbee, Jeffrey T., and Nancy A. Recchie. *Little Cities of Black Diamonds*. Charleston SC: Arcadia, 2009.

"History of Ohio Coal Mining." Ohio Coal Association. October 23, 2019. www.ohiocoal.com.

Hulbert, Archer Butler, ed. *The Records of the Original Proceedings of the Ohio Company*. Marietta GA: Marietta Historical Commission, 1917.

"Murray City, Ohio Train Depot and Coal Mining Museum." murraycitydepot.com (site discontinued).

"Policing the Plasma Plants." *Time*, August 17, 1970.

"San Toy, the Town that Ain't No More: Ghost Town of Morgan and Perry Counties." McConnelsville OH: Morgan County Historical Society, 1987.

Shaefer, Luke H., and Analidis Ochoa. "How Blood-Plasma Companies Target the Poorest Americans." *The Atlantic*, March 15, 2018.

Tribe, Ivan M. *An Empire of Industry: Hocking Valley Mining Towns in the Gilded Age*. Toledo OH: University of Toledo. 1976.

————. *Sprinkled with Coal Dust: Life and Work in the Hocking Coal Region, 1870–1900*. Athens OH: Athens County Historical Society and Museum, 1989.

Walker, Charles. *The History of Athens County, Ohio*. Cincinnati OH: Robert Clarke, 1869.

White Trash

I can't say enough about Nancy Isenberg's *White Trash: The 400-Year Untold History of Class in America*. My essay is as much a critical and creative response to that book as anything. And Isenberg's work pairs nicely with "The Case for Reparations," by Ta-Nehisi Coates, published in *The Atlantic*. And if those two aren't enough, consider *Dream Hoarders* by Richard Reeves, which spends an entire book rethinking social mobility in ways that I only hint at in my essay.

Adams, James Truslow. *The Epic of America*. New York: Clue Ribbon Books, 1931.

Buchholz, Henrich E. *Of What Use Are Common People*. West Warwick RI: Warwick & Work, 1923.

Galenson, David W. *White Servitude in Colonial America*. Cambridge: Cambridge University Press, 1981.

Hepp, John Henry, IV. *The Middle-Class City*. Philadelphia: University of Pennsylvania Press, 2003.

Huber, Joan, and William H. Form. *Income and Ideology*. New York: Free Press, 1973.

Isenberg, Nancy. *White Trash. The 400-Year Untold History of Class in America*. New York: Viking, 2016.

Jensen, Barbara. *Reading Classes: On Culture and Classism in America*. Ithaca NY: Cornell University Press, 2012.

Jordan, Don, and Michael Walsh. *White Cargo: The Forgotten History of Britain's White Slaves in America*. New York: New York University Press, 2007.

Moore, Wes. *The Other*. New York: Spiegel & Grau, 2010.

Morgan, Kenneth. *Slavery and Servitude in Colonial North America*. New York: New York University Press, 2001.

Murray, Charles. *Human Accomplishment*. New York: HarperCollins, 2003.

Neill, Edward D. *History of the Virginia Company of London, with Letters to and from the First Colony Never Before Printed*. New York: Burt Franklin, 1968.

Reeves, Richard V. *Dream Hoarders: How the American Upper Middle Class Is Leaving Everyone Else in the Dust, Why That Is a Problem, and What to Do about It*. Washington DC: Brookings Institution Press, 2017.

Rodriguez, Gregory. *Mongrels, Bastards, Orphans, and Vagabonds*. New York: Pantheon Books, 2007.

Salinger, Sharon V. *"To Serve Well and Faithfully" Labor and Indentured Servants in Pennsylvania, 1682–1800*. Cambridge: Cambridge University Press, 1987.

Smith, Abbot Emerson. *Colonists in Bondage*. Chapel Hill: University of North Carolina Press, 1947.

Smith, Warren B. *White Servitude in Colonial South Carolina*. Columbia: University of South Carolina Press, 1961.

Stokes, Mason. *The Color of Sex*. Durham NC: Duke University Press, 2001.

Strasser, Susan. *Waste and Want*. New York: Metropolitan Books, 1999.

Van Cleve, George William. *A Slaveholders' Union*. Chicago: University of Chicago Press, 2010.

Weidensaul, Scott. *The First Frontier*. Boston: Houghton Mifflin Harcourt, 2012.

Not in My Backyard

I could not have retold the story of Tent City without the excellent reporting of several local journalists in Lubbock. In particular, I would like to acknowledge the work of Elliott Blackburn, Shelly Gonzalez, Tiffany Pelt, Christie Post, Cole Shooter, Adam Young, and others at the Lubbock Avalanche-Journal, KCBD News Channel 11, and KFYO FM 750, whose stories helped me put together a timeline of Tent City's development. Their hours of on-the-scene reporting has provided Lubbock with an invaluable record of local homelessness issues.

Angotti, Tom. "The Seventh Generation: How Smarth [*sic*] Growth Can Save Growth." The Organization of Progressive Planners, March 27, 2012. www.plannersnetwork.org.

Archibold, Randal C. "Las Vegas Makes It Illegal to Feed Homeless in Parks." *New York Times*, July 28, 2006.

Bianchi, Mike. "Jacksonville's Homeless Just Super, For Now." *Orlando Sentinel*, February 5, 2005. www.orlandosentinel.com.

Blackburn, Elliott. "Council Won't Create New Committee to Study Homelessness." *Lubbock Avalanche Journal*, February 24, 2010. www.lubbockonline.com.

———. "Lubbock City Council Creates Homeless Committee." *Lubbock Avalanche-Journal*, October 28, 2010. www.lubbockonline.com.

———. "Lubbock Council Rejects Committee on Homelessness." *Lubbock Avalanche-Journal*, February 26, 2010. www.lubbockonline.com.

———. "Lubbock Residents Address Concerns over Homeless." *Lubbock Avalanche-Journal*, October 22, 2010. www.lubbockonline.com.

Bumiller, Elisabeth. "In Wake of Attack, Giuliani Cracks Down on Homeless." *New York Times*, November 20, 1999. www.nytimes.com.

Clifton, Blake, MD. Personal Interview. April 14, 2012.

Duke Today Staff. "A Brain's Failure to Appreciate Others May Permit Human Atrocities." Duke University, December 14, 2011. www.today.duke.edu.

Har, Janie. "Portland Mayor Makes City's Third Try at Regulating Panhandlers." *The Oregonian*, March 24, 2010. www.oregonlive.com.

"Hats Off: Ministry Comes to the Rescue with New Site for Homeless' Tent Camp." *Lubbock Avalanche-Journal*, March 11, 2011. www.lubbockonline.com.

"Homelessness & Poverty in America." National Law Center on Poverty and Homelessness, 2012. www.nlchp.org.

"Intense Cold Front Produces Severe Winds and Blowing Dust—17 October 2011." National Weather Service, January 3, 2012. www.weather.gov.

Kenney, Nick. "Understanding Memphis' Panhandling Ordinance." Action News 5, April 14, 2010. www.wmcactionnews5.com.

Kramer, Eric Mark, and Soobum Lee. "Homelessness: The Other as Object." *Reading the Homeless*. Edited by Eungjun Min. Westport CT: Praeger, 1999.

Morris, Desmond. *The Human Zoo*. New York: Kodansha, 1996. Previously published 1969 by McGraw-Hill (New York).

Pelt, Tiffany. "Lubbock's Homeless Tent City Could Soon Be Shut Down." *Lubbock Avalanche-Journal*, September 5, 2011. www.lubbockonline.com.

———. "Proposed Ordinances Take Aim at Homeless near Library." News Channel 11, October 26, 2010. www.kcbd.com.

Post, Christie. "Council Votes Unanimously to Keep Tent City." KCBD News Channel 11, October 27, 2011. www.kcbd.com.

———. "Tent City More than Doubles in One Month, Now Facing Relocation." KCBD News Channel 11, February 23, 2011. www.kcbd.com.

———. "Tent City Struggles to Rebuild after Epic Dust Storm." KCBD News Channel 11, October 19, 2011. www.kcbd.com.

Pritchett, Rachel. "Neighbors Object to Proposed Homeless Camp in East Bremerton." *Kitsap Sun*, October 11, 2010. www.kitsapsun.com.

Richey, Warren. "Orlando Can Restrict Feeding the Homeless, Rules 11th Circuit." *Christian Science Monitor*, April 12, 2011. www.csmonitor.com.

Shooter, Cole. "Lubbock Homelessness Committee Recommends No

Major Changes, Says Private Charities Address Issue." KFYO News
Talk FM 790, May 31, 2011. www.kfyo.com.

"User Code of Conduct." Lubbock Public Library, August 16, 2010.
www.library.ci.lubbock.tx.us.

Warsmith, Stephanie. "Council Considers Requiring Solicitors to Be
More than 100 Feet from Intersections for Safety Reasons." *Akron
Beacon Journal*, June 21, 2011. www.ohio.com.

Westaby, Robb. "Judge to Hear Challenge to Michigan Laws against
Panhandling." *Fox News Michigan*, February 16, 2012. www
.fox17online.com.

Young, Adam. "Loophole Allows Homeless to Camp on City Land." *Lubbock Avalanche-Journal*, February 20, 2011. www.lubbockonline.com.

———. "Troubles of Heat, Outdoor Life Tempered by Donations
for Tent Villagers." *Lubbock Avalanche-Journal*, July 17, 2011. www
.lubbockonline.com.

Young, Adam, and Shelly Gonzales. "Tent City Downtown Gets Notice
of Need to Move." *Lubbock Avalanche-Journal*, February 23, 2011.
www.lubbockonline.com.

The Full Montaigne

To read Montaigne or not to read him—that is the question. At least if you're a nerd for creative nonfiction. I took my first workshop on the essay from Patrick Madden and helped him develop quotidiana.org, an online anthology of classical essays, so I'm biased in favor of the Frenchman, but I understand the reticence of some readers. The English translations can be stodgy (though I can't read the original French, so those may be just as stodgy for all I know), and his views are sometimes dated in the ways you would expect from a privileged nobleman in the sixteenth century. And yet I keep coming back to him, the way I find myself coming back to the wisdom of scripture. There's something remarkable about the sheer heft of his work, the depth of his insights, the clarity of view. To me, reading Montaigne is like reading Shakespeare, or the psalmists. Everyone should take a crack at it but maybe not on the beach or before bed.

Lévinas, Emmanuel. *On Escape*. Stanford: Stanford University Press, 2003.

Lopate, Phillip. *Portrait of My Body*. New York: Anchor, 1996.

Miller, Brenda. "Body Language." In *Seasons of the Body*, edited by Brenda Miller. Louisville KY: Sarabande, 2002.

Montaigne, Michel de. "Of the Custom of Wearing Clothes." In *Essays of Michel de Montaigne*, translated by Charles Cotton, edited by William Carew Hazlitt. London, 1877. Project Gutenberg, 2006. www .gutenberg.org.

———. "Of the Inequality Amoungst Us." In *Essays of Michel de Montaigne*, translated by Charles Cotton, edited by William Carew Hazlitt. London, 1877. Project Gutenberg, 2006. www.gutenberg.org.

———. "On Some Verses of Virgil." In *Essays of Michel de Montaigne*, translated by Charles Cotton, edited by William Carew Hazlitt. London, 1877. Project Gutenberg, 2006. www.gutenberg.org.

———. "That to Study Philosophy Is to Learn to Die." In *Essays of Michel de Montaigne*, translated by Charles Cotton, edited by William Carew Hazlitt. London, 1877. Project Gutenberg, 2006. www .gutenberg.org.

———. "To the Reader." In *Essays of Michel de Montaigne*, translated by Charles Cotton, edited by William Carew Hazlitt. London, 1877. Project Gutenberg, 2006. www.gutenberg.org.

Sanders, Scott Russell. "Singular First Person." In *Essays on the Essay*, edited by Alexander J. Butrym. Athens: University of Georgia Press, 1989.

White, E. B. *Letters of E. B. White*. Rev. ed. New York: HarperCollins, 2006.

———. "Once More to the Lake." In *Essays of E. B. White*. New York: Harper Perennial, 1999.

Woolfolk, R. L., and F. Richardson. *Sanity, Stress and Survival*. New York: Signet, 1978.

Worry Lines

Brian Doyle once wrote: "If we ever forget that there is something in us beyond sense and reason that snarls at death and runs roaring at it to defend children, if we ever forget that all children are our children, then we are fools who have allowed memory to be murdered too, and what good are we then?" I have admired the way Sybrina Fulton and Tracy Martin have worked so tirelessly to infuse the memory of their son with power, and I hope that this essay contributes to that work in a small way.

Adler, Ben. "Conservative Media Smears Trayvon Martin." *The Nation*, March 27, 2012. www.thenation.com.

"Audio: Calls from Zimmerman, Neighbor Capture Last Minutes of Martin's Life." *Washington Post*, September 10, 2019. www.washingtonpost.com.

Baldwin, James. "On Being 'White' . . . and Other Lies." In *Black on White: Black Writers on What It Means to Be White*, edited by David R. Roediger. New York: Schocken Books, 1998.

Boehlert, Eric. "Trayvon Martin and Why the Right-Wing Media Spent 16 Months Smearing a Dead Teenager." Media Matters for America, July 17, 2013. www.mediamatters.org.

Brandon-Croft, Barbara. "Raising a Black Boy in America." *Parents*. www.parents.com.

Brown, Sherronda J. "Decolonizing Empathy: Why Our Pain Will Never Be Enough to Disarm White Supremacy." Black Youth Project, November 13, 2017. www.blackyouthproject.com.

Coates, Ta-Nehisi. *Between the World and Me*. New York: Random House, 2015.

DiAngelo, Robin. *What Does It Mean to Be White?* Pieterlen and Bern, Switzerland: Peter Lang, 2012.

DuBois, W. E. B. "Criteria of Negro Art." *The Crisis*, October 1926, 290–97. www.webdubois.org.

———. "Of Our Spiritual Strivings." In *The Soul of Black Folk*. Chicago: A. C. McClurg, 1902.

Dwyer, Liz. "'Is My Child Next?': How Raising Black Kids Is Affecting Our Mental Health." Shondaland, August 1, 2018. www.shondaland.com.

Francescani, Chris. "George Zimmerman: Prelude to a Shooting." Discover Thomson Reuters, April 25, 2012. www.reuters.com.

Fulton, Sybrina, and Tracy Martin. *Rest in Power*. New York: Spiegel & Grau, 2017.

Murphy, Laura. "A Mother's Rules for Being Young, Black, and Male." ACLU, July 18, 2013. www.aclu.org/blog.

Rankine, Claudia. *Citizen*. Minneapolis MN: Graywolf, 2014.

Robles, Frances. "Shooter of Trayvon Martin a Habitual Caller to Cops." *Miami Herald*, March 17, 2012. www.miamiherald.com.

Apocalypse, Now?

Years after first spotting that "In case of rapture, this car will be empty" bumper sticker, I saw another one that read, "In case of rapture, can I have your car?" I appreciate this take on the Apocalypse, partly because the first bumper sticker seems so presumptuous. But also because I love the pedestrian notion of some poor damned soul left out of the rapture, giddy with all the free stuff left behind. More than that though, the second bumper sticker suggests a necessary criticism. In the real, complex world of human problems, abandoning ship is rarely a helpful solution.

Al-Haddad, Haitham. "Reasons behind the Japanese Tsunami." Islam21c, March 15, 2011. www.islam21c.com.

Bahr, Fax, George Hickenlooper, Eleanor Coppola, and Francis Ford

Coppola. *Hearts of Darkness: A Filmmaker's Apocalypse*. American
Zoetrope, 2017. DVD.

Chang, Kenneth. "Quake Moves Japan Closer to U.S. and Alters Earth's
Spin." *New York Times*, March 13, 2011.

Coppola, Eleanor. *Notes*. New York City: Pocket Books, 1979.

Coppola, Francis Ford, John Milius, Marlon Brando, Robert Duvall,
Martin Sheen, Frederic Forrest, Albert Hall, et al. *Apocalypse Now*.
Miramax, 1999. DVD.

Doyle, Brian. "A Sin." In *Grace Notes*. Calgary, Canada: Acta, 2011.

Fenn, Richard K. *Dreams of Glory: The Sources of Apocalyptic Terror*.
Farnham, UK: Ashgate, 2006.

Himmelfarb, Martha. *The Apocalypse: A Brief History*. New Jersey:
Wiley-Blackwell, 2010.

"Jesus Will Return by 2050, Say 40pc of Americans." *The Telegraph*, June
22, 2010. www.telegraph.co.uk.

Keller, Catherine. *Apocalypse Now and Then*. Boston: Beacon, 1996.

Lamb, Charles. "New Year's Eve." In *The Essays of Elia*. New York City:
Little, Brown, 1892.

Marikar, Sheila. "Glenn Beck Calls Japan Earthquake Work of God;
Gilbert Gottfried Apologizes." ABC News, March 15, 2011. abcnews
.go.com.

McCants, William. *The ISIS Apocalypse: The History, Strategy, and
Doomsday Vision of the Islamic State Paperback*. New York: Picador,
2016.

McCurry, Justin. "Tokyo Governor Apologizes for Calling Tsunami 'Divine Punishment.'" *The Guardian*, March 15, 2011. www
.theguardian.com.

McFate, Jessica Lewis. "The ISIS Defense in Iraq and Syria: Countering
an Adaptive Enemy." *Middle East Security Report* 27 (May 2015): 11.
Institute for the Study of War. www.understandingwar.org.

McIver, Tom. *The End of the World: An Annotated Bibliography*. Jefferson
NC: McFarland, 1999.

Oskin, Becky. "Japan Earthquake & Tsunami of 2011: Facts and Information." Live Science, September 13, 2017. www.livescience.com.

Rawles, Timothy. "Pastor Blames CA Wildfires on Gay People in Text-
   books." *San Diego Gay and Lesbian News*, January 5, 2018. sdgln.com.

Rubinsky, Yuri, and Ian Wiseman. *A History of the End of the World.*
   New York: William Morrow, 1982.

"Russian Director Says Tsunami Sent to Punish 'Godless' People." *The
   Observers.* Aired March 23, 2011. www.observers.france24.com.

Shae, Danny. "Pat Robertson: Haiti 'Cursed' by 'Pact to the Devil.'"
   Huffpost, March 3, 2010. www.huffpost.com.

Shiraiwa, Yoko. "Rescuing Tsunami-Damaged Photographs in Japan."
   Journal of the Institute of Conservation 36, no. 2 (2013): 195–203.

Yeats, William Butler. "The Second Coming." Poetry Foundation, 1989.
   www.poetryfoundation.org.

A Note on Notes

If I quote someone here, I risk the need for a note to my note on
"A Note on Notes," which reminds me of the 1929 Hilaire Belloc meta-meta essay titled "An Essay upon Essays upon Essays,"
but as this back matter is already overdue to my publisher, I'll
refrain. Though I would recommend the Belloc essay, if only to
introduce you to this great line: "There is no reason why a fairly
well-read [person], still active and enjoying occasional travel, let
alone the infinite experience of daily life, should lack a subject.
Stuff is infinite. The danger lies not in the drying up of matter
but in the fossilization of manner." There, I quoted him anyway.
You'll have to google that one, but here are the other sources from
my "Note on Notes":

Carr, Nicholas. "Is Google Making Us Stupid?" *The Atlantic*, July/
   August 2008. www.theatlantic.com.

Gass, William H. "Emerson and the Essay." In *Habitations of the Word: Essays*, 9–49. New York: Simon and Schuster, 1985.

Lopate, Phillip. Introduction to *The Art of the Personal Essay*, xli. New York: Anchor, 1994.

Monson, Ander. "Essay as Hack." Other Electricities. www.otherelectricities.com.

Montaigne, Michel de. "Of Books." In *Essays of Michel de Montaigne*, translated by Charles Cotton, edited by William Carew Hazlitt. London, 1877. Project Gutenberg, 2006. www.gutenberg.org.

CPSIA information can be obtained
at www.ICGtesting.com
Printed in the USA
LVHW111112260820
664281LV00001B/352

9 781496 212108